IN PURSUIT OF

BIBLE TRIVIA

BELIEVERS EDITION
SECOND VOLUME

Bob Phillips

HARVEST HOUSE PUBLISHERS
Eugene, Oregon 97402

IN PURSUIT OF BIBLE TRIVIA—SECOND VOLUME

Copyright © 1985 by Harvest House Publishers
Eugene, Oregon 97402

Library of Congress Catalog Card Number 84-82351
ISBN 0-89081-464-3

Printed in the United States of America.

To Richard Hanson and David Ferreira...
who have put up with all of my humor and trivia
and remain true friends.

Table of Contents

Introduction

As a result of my first trivia book, I have had many friends and interested folk share their appreciation. They have also suggested additional trivia questions of their own and encouraged me to compile a second volume. This interest, coupled with the encouragement of Bob Hawkins at Harvest House Publishers, has led to the second volume of *In Pursuit of Bible Trivia.*

This volume expands my collection of unusual Bible facts. These tidbits of trivia can be shared with your friends and add sparkle to sermons and group gatherings. Also included is a section of humorous Bible puns and riddles. Special additions in this edition are two unique readings entitled "Melody in F" and "The Christ of the Bible."

In Pursuit of Bible Trivia can be utilized in a number of different ways:

- You can read it just for your own personal amusement and review of your Bible knowledge. It is designed in such a way that you can write down your answers to the questions.
- You can use the unusual facts to add interest and humor to your public speaking.
- You can use the book as a tool to help pass the time while traveling as a family. Many of the facts will spark discussion about Bible events and stories.
- You can utilize the little-known facts as an icebreaker at various get-togethers.
- You can take various questions in the book and use them as part of a biblical pursuit game with a small group of friends.
- You can share the questions on a large group or team basis also. Questions along with the answers are repeated in the back of the book. This was done in the event you would like to ask questions of a group

and have an immediate answer ready. You will find a large group game like this to be much fun for everyone.

As you answer the questions of *In Pursuit of Bible Trivia*, I hope that you will find them educational and fun. If that is done, my purpose in writing will have been accomplished.

—Bob Phillips
Hume, California

IN PURSUIT
OF
BIBLE
TRIVIA

■ *Easy Trivia Questions*

1. What was the name of the garden Jesus prayed in?

   _____

2. In what book of the Bible do we read about God's armor?

   _____

3. "Without the _____ _____ _____ there is no forgiveness" (NIV).

4. How many demons did Mary Magdalene have in her?
   a. Two   b. Three   c. Five   d. Seven   e. Nine

5. How old was the daughter of Jairus?

   _____

6. What book comes before 1 Kings?

   _____

7. What are the names of the two men who had a sharp argument over John Mark?

   _____

8. Which chapter in the Bible lists the heroes of faith?

   _____

9. What Bible character stood on Mars Hill?

_____

10. "With God all things are _____."

11. A man who has his quiver full of them is happy. What is in the quiver?

_____

12. Who was the first person to experience fear in the Bible?

_____

13. "_____ _____ is the same yesterday and today and forever" (NIV).

14. Peter says that in the last days_____will come.

15. Who shut the door on Noah's Ark?

_____

16. What time of day did Adam and Eve hear God walking in the Garden of Eden?

_____

17. Who said, "I will exalt my throne above the stars of God"?

_____

18. What Bible character talks about "the twinkling of an eye"?

_____

19. Who was the first person in the Bible to take a nap?

_____

20. Paul prayed _____ times to have his thorn in the flesh removed.

21. Quote Romans 3:23.

_____

22. What Bible character said, "Where your treasure is, there will your heart be also"?

_____

23. What is the book just before Micah?

_____

24. Into how many pieces was Jesus' seamless garment cut?

_____

25. In what book of the Bible does it talk about 100-pound (or a talent) hailstones?

_____

26. Who had a spear with the iron head weighing 600 shekels?

_____

27. In what chapter of the Bible do we find Jesus' high priestly prayer?

_____

28. The Egyptians thought Sarah was related to Abraham in what way?

_____

29. Which tribe of Israel had the responsibility of moving the tabernacle?

_____

30. What book comes after the book of Obadiah?

_____

31. What is the first word in the Bible?

_____

32. In what chapter of the Bible do you find the phrase, "He leadeth me beside the still waters"?

_____

33. God told Adam and Eve not to eat what kind of fruit?

   _____

34. "_____ goeth before destruction, and a haughty spirit before a fall."

35. When Jesus was 12 He was unintentionally left behind by Mary and Joseph. How many days did they look for Him?

   _____

36. How many times a year did the high priest enter the Holy of Holies to make atonement for all the sins of Israel?

   _____

37. Who said, "Naked I came from my mother's womb" (NIV)?

   _____

38. How old was Jesus when it was first mentioned that He went to Jerusalem for the Passover?

   _____

39. How many men believed in Christ after Peter's second sermon?

   _____

40. "For the wages of sin is _____, but the gift of God is _____ _____" (NIV).

41. Two Old Testament cities were destroyed because of their great wickedness. What were their names?

   _____

42. In the Garden of Gethsemane, Jesus sweat great drops of _____.

43. The Bible suggests that a thousand years in God's sight is as how long?

   _____

44. Who said, "Foxes have holes and birds of the air have nests" (NIV)?

_____

45. Which of the 12 disciples was in charge of the money?

_____

46. What book comes before the book of Lamentations?

_____

47. Who said, "Before Abraham was born, I am" (NIV)?

_____

48. In what book of the Bible do we find the quotation, "God helps those who help themselves"?

_____

49. What is the name of the disciple who took care of Jesus' mother after His death?

_____

50. Quote Philippians 4:4.

_____

51. What book comes before the book of Isaiah?

_____

52. What Bible character said, "What must I do to be saved?"

_____

53. How many chapters are there in the book of Jude?

_____

54. Who asked Jesus, "Are you the king of the Jews?" (NIV).

_____

55. "Trust in the Lord with all thine _____; and lean not unto thine own _____."

56. When the Philistines finally captured Samson, what did they do to him?

_____

57. What was the first thing that Adam and Eve did after they sinned?

_____

58. "For nothing is _____ with God" (NIV).

59. What are the names of the two Bible characters who did not die?

_____

60. "For by grace are ye _____ through _____; and that not of yourselves: it is the gift of God."

61. Peter suggests that the day of the Lord will come as a _____.

62. What Bible character said, "I am a man of unclean lips"?

_____

63. What chapter of the Bible is considered the love chapter?

_____

64. "The_____says in his heart, 'There is no _____' " (NIV).

65. On the seventh day of creation, what did God do?

_____

66. Who told the first lie in the Bible?

_____

67. When Jesus healed the ten lepers, how many returned and thanked Him?

_____

68. How many days did it take Nehemiah to inspect the city walls of Jerusalem before rebuilding them?

_____

69. Quote John 1:12.

_____

70. What was the home town of King David?

_____

71. What book comes after the book of Malachi?

_____

72. John wrote the book of Revelation on what island?

_____

73. How many chapters are there in the book of Colossians?

_____

74. In what book of the Bible do we find the words, "Abstain from all appearance of evil"?

_____

75. On what mountains did Noah's Ark come to rest?

_____

76. What are the names of the two men who wrapped Jesus' body for burial?

_____

77. The poor widow in the book of Luke put how many coins into the temple treasury?

_____

78. In what book of the Bible do we find the phrase, "The very hairs of your head are all numbered"?

_____

79. Who is the author of the book of Zephaniah?

_____

80. Who was the first person to enter the empty tomb of Jesus?

_____

81. Isaiah compares our righteousness to _____ _____.

82. What is the number of the beast in the book of Revelation?

_____

83. In what book of the Bible do we find the phrase, "Give us this day our daily bread"?

_____

84. Who succeeded Moses as leader of the children of Israel?

_____

85. In what book of the Bible do we find the words, "Without the shedding of blood there is no forgiveness"?

_____

86. Who disguises himself as an angel of light?

_____

87. When David was a boy, what two fierce animals did he kill?

_____

88. How many years will Satan be bound in the Abyss (bottomless pit)?

_____

89. What was the name of the type of leaf that Adam and Eve wore before the fall?

_____

90. What Bible character originally said, "It is more blessed to give than to receive" (NIV)?

_____

91. Name the first five people mentioned in the Bible.

_____

92. How many of the sacrifice sheep did Moses take into the Ark with him?

_____

93. Lydia is known for selling what?

_____

94. What does the Bible say has never been tamed by man?

_____

95. The Bible says there is one thing that never fails. What is it?

_____

96. In what book of the Bible do we find the words, "For my yoke is easy and my burden is light"?

_____

97. How many times is the word Bible used in the Bible?

_____

98. What book comes after the book of Micah?

_____

99. "For where your _____ is, there your _____ will be also" (NIV).

100. What book comes after the book of Hebrews?

_____

101. On what two parts of the body will the mark of the beast be placed?

_____

102. In what book of the Bible do you find the words born again?

_____

103. In what book of the Bible is the verse, "Cleanliness is next to godliness"?

_____

104. Jonah purchased his boat ticket in what city?

_____

105. "I can do all things through _____ who _____ me."

106. What are the names of the three disciples who were the shortest distance from Jesus in Gethsemane while He prayed?

_____

107. In what book of the Bible do we find the words, "If any of you lack wisdom, let him ask of God"?

_____

108. What is the name of the disciple who was instructed to touch the nail prints in Jesus' hands after His resurrection?

_____

109. What was the name of the angel who spoke to Mary the mother of Jesus?

_____

110. Judas agreed to betray Jesus for how many pieces of silver?

_____

111. What Bible character said, "How can a man be born when he is old?"

_____

112. Who does the Bible say holds the keys of hell and death?

_____

113. What were the names of the two sisters of Lazarus?

_____

114. What kind of valley is described in Psalm 23?

_____

115. What Bible character put out a fleece to test God?

_____

■ *Fairly Easy Trivia Questions*

1. Who was the first Bible character to use a riddle?

   _____

2. What was the New Testament word for teacher?

   _____

3. What is the name of the man who carried Jesus' cross?

   _____

4. In order for a man to become a bond slave, what did he have to do?

   _____

5. In speaking of Jesus, who said, "Certainly this was a righteous man"?

   _____

6. How many men did Nebuchadnezzar see walking in the fiery furnace?

   _____

7. In what book of the Bible do we read the words, "Whoso

findeth a wife findeth a good thing"?

---

8. What was the name of the Bible character who put a veil over his face to hide the glory of God?

---

9. Jesus was a descendant of what tribe of Israel?

---

10. Saul had a troubled spirit that could only be soothed by _____.

11. The disciples were first called Christians in what city?

---

12. What book comes before the book of Joel?

---

13. Who prayed the shortest prayer recorded in the Bible?

---

14. Quote the shortest prayer in the Bible.

---

15. What Bible character said, "What a wretched man I am" (NIV)?

---

16. What man in the Bible was called the Son of Encouragement (or consolation)?

---

17. Quote Isaiah 53:6.

---

18. In what book of the Bible do we read the words, "Your attitude should be the same as that of Christ Jesus" (NIV)?

---

19. "Believe on the Lord Jesus Christ, and thou shalt be

    _____, and thy _____."

20. In what book of the Bible do we read the words, "What-soever a man soweth, that shall he also reap"?

    _____

21. What does Proverbs 22 suggest is more desirable than great riches?

    _____

22. What is the name of the first Bible character mentioned drinking wine?

    _____

23. What is the number of the largest group of people to whom Christ appeared after His resurrection?

    _____

24. Name the three Bible characters who are mentioned as fasting for 40 days.

    _____

25. List the books of the Bible that are named after women.

    _____

26. Quote Philippians 1:21.

    _____

27. If a man hates his son, he will not bother to do what?

    _____

28. Which book comes before the book of Obadiah?

    _____

29. What Bible character said, "Here am I; send me"?

    _____

30. The country of Lebanon is famous for what kind of trees?

    _____

31. _____ was called God's friend.

32. According to Timothy, what will people love in the last days?

_____

33. At the time of Christ's birth, who issued a decree for a census (NIV) or tax (KJV)?

_____

34. In what book of the Bible do we find the words, "Every man did that which was right in his own eyes"?

_____

35. What book comes after the book of Habakkuk?

_____

36. How many days after Jesus' resurrection did He ascend to heaven?

_____

37. What Bible character called her husband master (lord)?

_____

38. Name the Bible character who was buried by God.

_____

39. According to 2 Timothy, Scripture is profitable for four things. What are they?

_____

40. What was the name of the father of James and John?

_____

41. Did Hezekiah author the book of Hezekiah?

_____

42. Jesus told His disciples in the book of Acts that they would be witnesses in three specific locations. What were those locations?

_____

43. What did the rich man in hell want?

_____

44. Quote 1 Thessalonians 5:16.

_____

45. How did God punish Eve for sinning in the Garden of Eden?

_____

46. In the book of Romans, God is quoted as hating what Bible character?

_____

47. Ananias was told to go to a street called _____.

48. When Joshua entered the Promised Land, what was the name of the second city he attacked?

_____

49. Who was the first man to suggest that Jonah be thrown overboard as a result of the storm?

_____

50. What was the name of the Bible character who because of his age slept with a beautiful young virgin in order to keep warm?

_____

51. Which church in the book of Revelation was called lukewarm?

_____

52. When the Israelites complained about eating only manna, what did God do?

_____

53. Who was the prophet Samuel speaking to when he said, "To obey is better than sacrifice"?

_____

54. In the book of Acts, how many men were chosen to wait on tables?

_____

55. What is the name of the man who wanted to buy the ability to do miracles like Peter and John?

_____

56. Who were the first twins mentioned in the Bible?

_____

57. Quote Philippians 4:13.

_____

58. What was the name of Adam's son who replaced Abel?

_____

59. How did the prophet Elijah travel to heaven?

_____

60. Which two New Testament books instruct husbands to love their wives?

_____

61. After Dinah was raped by Shechem, what did her brothers do?

_____

62. In what book of the Bible do we find the words, "Though your sins are like scarlet, they shall be as white as snow" (NIV)?

_____

63. King Herod was eaten by _____.

64. In the Old Testament, murderers could flee to what cities in order to be safe?

_____

65. Which disciple objected to Mary washing Jesus' feet with perfume?

66. What is the eighth book of the Bible?

67. To whom was Paul speaking when he said, "Let no man despise thy youth"?

68. What is the name of the Pharisee who defended the apostles before the Sanhedrin in the book of Acts?

69. Who were the first Gentiles in Caesarea to be converted to Christianity?

70. What is the name of the queen for whom the Ethiopian eunuch worked?

71. Which is the longest book in the New Testament?
    a. Matthew   b. Luke   c. Romans   d. Revelation

72. What is the name of the Bible character who said, "Let me inherit a double portion of your spirit" (NIV)?

73. When Philip met the Ethiopian eunuch, he was reading from the book of which prophet?

74. Quote 1 Thessalonians 5:18.

75. In the book of Philemon, what is the name of the servant for whom Paul was making an appeal?

76. What were the names of Job's three friends?

_____

77. As a result of Adam's sin, what became cursed?

_____

78. Who does James suggest will be judged more strictly than others?

_____

79. What is the name of the man whom King David made drunk?

_____

80. The book of Romans has how many chapters?

_____

81. Lydia, the seller of purple, was from which city?

_____

82. In what book of the Bible did Paul state that people who do not work should not eat?

_____

83. What New Testament book tells the story of a man eating a book (or scroll)?

_____

84. In what book of the Bible does it talk about Satan accusing believers before God day and night?

_____

85. In the book of Acts, what was the name of the man who predicted that a famine would spread over the entire Roman world?

_____

86. What does Proverbs say is a mocker?

_____

87. The word Armageddon is used only one time in Scripture. In what book of the Bible is this word found?

_____

88. In what book in the Bible does it suggest that we not eat too much honey?

_____

89. In the book of Colossians there was a man named Justus. What was his famous other name?

_____

90. Who was the first person mentioned in the Bible as laughing?

_____

91. What does the Bible say was put in charge to bring us to Christ before faith came?

_____

92. When David had to face Goliath, he picked up:
    a. Three rough stones   b. Five smooth stones
    c. Five rough stones   d. Three smooth stones

93. Which one of Noah's sons looked on Noah's nakedness?

_____

94. What is the name of the priest that Abram met in the valley of Shaveh?

_____

95. What is the name of the land that God told Abram to leave?

_____

96. In 1 Corinthians, what is the last enemy to be destroyed?

_____

97. Which of these did Jesus cure first?
    a. Blindness   b. Leprosy   c. Lameness

98. What was the name of the man who made a metal snake and put it on a pole?

   _____

99. In what book of the Bible do you find the words, "Remember your Creator in the days of your youth" (NIV)?

   _____

100. Quote Romans 8:28.

   _____

   _____

101. The book of Proverbs suggests that a good medicine is

   a _____ _____ .

102. When blind Bartimaeus came to Jesus, he threw something away. What was it?

   _____

103. An Israelite man was exempt from war for how long after he was married?

   _____

104. King Herod killed all the baby boys in Bethlehem who were

   _____ years old and under.

105. What was the name of an angel that fought with the dragon in the book of Revelation?

   _____

106. What was the name of Solomon's mother?

   _____

107. What did the angels do to the homosexual men of Sodom to protect Lot?

   _____

108. Why did Adam name his wife Eve?

   _____

109. Who said, "I am slow of speech, and of a slow tongue"?

110. What two things did God say would happen to Eve for disobedience in the Garden of Eden?

111. Who said there is "a time to weep and a time to laugh"?

112. In the book of Revelation, who held the key to the Abyss (bottomless pit)?

113. Who said, "How beautiful are the feet of them that preach the gospel of peace"?

114. Who wore golden bells on the hem of a blue robe?

115. What was the name of the Bible character who had red hair like a garment all over his body?

116. When Apollos came from Alexandria, he first preached in what city?

117. In what New Testament book do you find the words, "What therefore God hath joined together let not man put asunder"?

118. Philip had four daughters who had a special spiritual gift. What was that gift?

119. What is the name of the only man mentioned in the Bible as being bald-headed?

120. When the angel in the book of Revelation came to bind Satan, what two objects did he have in his hand?

_____

121. Jesus calls Himself the morning star in what book of the Bible?

_____

122. What Bible character describes his girlfriend's hair as a flock of goats descending from Gilead?

_____

123. After Jesus' trial, what color of robe was put on Him?

_____

124. Which book of the Bible says, "I would rather be a doorkeeper in the house of my God than dwell in the tents of the wicked" (NIV)?

_____

125. What is the thirtieth book of the Bible?

_____

126. Quote Philippians 4:19.

_____

_____

■ *Fairly Difficult Trivia Questions*

1. What is the name of the Bible character who went to visit the witch of Endor?

   _____

2. A Christian who returns to a life of sin is likened to which animals?

   _____

3. In what book of the Bible does it talk about blood running so deep that it reaches up to the bridles of horses?

   _____

4. The furnace into which Shadrach, Meshach, and Abednego were tossed was heated how many times hotter than usual?

   _____

5. How many times did Jacob bow as he approached Esau?

   _____

6. What were the names of the two believers who discipled Apollos?

   _____

7. What was the name of Mordecai's cousin whom he brought up?

_____

8. What is the name of the tree that stands on both sides of the river of the water of life in the book of Revelation?

_____

9. What is the name of the Bible character who got leprosy by sticking his hand inside his cloak?

_____

10. Jesus said He could call on His Father for how many legions of angels?

_____

11. What was the occupation of Jairus?

_____

12. In what two books of the Bible do we find the phrase, "Be not weary in well doing"?

_____

13. What was the first command the Bible mentions that God gave to Adam and Eve?

_____

14. What was the name of the Bible character who was called "mighty in the Scriptures"?

_____

15. The Year of Jubilee comes how often for the Israelites?

_____

16. What will the gates of the holy city be made of?

_____

17. How many bowls of water did Gideon squeeze out of his fleece?

_____

18. Satan smote Job with_____from the soles of his feet to the top of his head.

19. Who suggested that it is not wise to spend too much time at your neighbor's house?

20. What Bible character said, "Almost thou persuadest me to be a Christian"?

21. David took two things from Saul while he was asleep. What were they?

22. What is the name of the Bible character who took all of the gold articles out of Solomon's temple?

23. In what book of the Bible do we read the words, "It is required in stewards that a man be found faithful"?

24. Where did Job live?
    a. Puz   b. Buz   c. Uz   d. Luz   e. Zuz

25. What was the name of Elisha's servant?

26. In what book of the Bible do we find the story about the sun standing still?

27. Which men wanted to kill Lazarus?

28. What color was manna?
    a. Yellowish   b. Reddish   c. Brownish   d. White

29. What two items that touched Paul were used then to heal people?

30. In the Promised Land there were_____cities of refuge.

31. Where does the Bible suggest that too much study is hard on the body?

    _____

32. Ruth and Boaz had a son named _____.

33. In what book of the Bible do we find the words, "He who wins souls is wise" (NIV)?

    _____

34. Zacchaeus repaid to the people he had cheated how many times the amount?

    _____

35. Name the New Testament book that was written to Gaius.

    _____

36. In what book of the Bible do we read the words, "For the love of money is the root of all evil"?

    _____

37. The poles used in carrying the Ark of the Covenant were made out of what kind of wood?

    _____

38. What was the other name of the Bible character called Didymus?

    _____

39. Who is the judge and defender of widows?

    _____

40. Does the Bible say that husbands should submit to their wives?

    _____

41. Who said that the Jews had holes in their purses?

    _____

42. Who is likened to a gold ring in a pig's snout?

43. At what time of day did Eutychus go to sleep and fall out of the window?

44. In what book of the Bible do you find the words, "It is more blessed to give than to receive"?

45. What two men were candidates for the position of the twelfth apostle after Judas' death?

46. What is the name of the man who replaced Judas as the twelfth apostle?

47. Earthly treasures are destroyed by three things. What are they?

48. In what book of the Bible do you find the words, "Man looks at the outward appearance, but the Lord looks at the heart" (NIV)?

49. According to Proverbs, the tongue of the wise brings what?

50. At what time of day is it not good to loudly bless your neighbor?

51. How many horns did the goat in Daniel's second vision have?

52. What was the name of Moses' father?

_____

53. Who said, "But godliness with contentment is great gain"?

_____

54. In what book of the Bible are we told to cast our bread upon the waters?

_____

55. What was the name of the boy who was left under a bush to die?

_____

56. In order to be on the church widow's list, how old did a widow need to be?

_____

57. What was on each of the four corners of the bronze altar in the tabernacle?

_____

58. The book of 1 Chronicles spends most of its pages discussing which Bible character?

_____

59. King Og's bed was made of what kind of metal?
    a. Gold   b. Iron   c. Silver   d. Steel   e. Brass

60. Paul asked Timothy to bring him two items while he was in prison. What were those items?

_____

61. What woman in the Bible faked a rape because she was mad?

_____

62. What was Tabitha's other name?

_____

63. What did Jesus and His disciples cross just before He was arrested?

_____

64. What does the Bible say cannot be bought for any price?

_____

65. The Bible says that male babies should be circumcised when they are how old?

_____

66. What is the name of the servant girl who answered the door when Peter escaped from prison?

_____

67. In the story of the rich man and Lazarus, how many brothers did the rich man have?

_____

68. How old was Isaac when he married Rebekah?

_____

69. When the kings of the East march westward, what river will dry up?

_____

70. What does "manna" mean?

_____

71. What are the names of the two women who fought over who would eat mandrakes?

_____

72. Where was the only place a Nazarite could cut his hair?

_____

73. The book of Proverbs names four things that are stately in their stride. What are they?

_____

74. In the book of Acts, Peter had a vision that repeated itself how many times?

_____

75. In the book of Revelation, what spice did the merchants of the earth sell to Babylon?

_____

76. Paul the apostle was stoned in what city?

_____

77. What is the name of the man who was ready to kill his son because he ate honey?

_____

78. What is the name of the man who was to provide for the needs of Mephibosheth?

_____

79. Manoah had a famous son. What was his name?

_____

80. When Abimelech set fire to the tower of Shechem, how many people died in the flames?

_____

81. Who does the Bible say goes around and whispers, peeps, and mutters?

_____

82. In what book of the Bible do we find mention of a mother eagle stirring up her nest?

_____

83. Who was the first person mentioned in the Bible as being put into prison?

_____

84. In which book of the Bible do we find mention of a synagogue of Satan?

_____

85. In the Old Testament, what particular people could not "make baldness upon their head" or cut off the edges of their beards?

86. Who said that we should not curse rich people from our bedroom?

87. How many times is the phrase "born again" mentioned in the Bible?

88. How many times does the word trinity appear in the Bible?

89. What Bible character fell on his face and laughed?

90. What Bible character said that laughter is mad (or foolish— NIV)?

91. Who said that even in laughter the heart is sorrowful (aches)?

92. In what book of the Bible does it say that, "A feast is made for laughter"?

93. What Bible character said, "Let your laughter be turned to mourning"?

94. What Bible character said, "The fear of the Lord, that is wisdom; and to depart from evil is understanding"?

95. What caused the flood waters to recede from the face of the earth?

_____

96. How many years did Noah live after the flood?

_____

97. What kind of grain did Boaz give to Ruth?

_____

98. In the book of Exodus, what was the color of the priest's robe?

_____

99. Saul was hiding in the _____ when he was to be presented as the king of Israel.

100. What was the name of Aaron's wife?

_____

101. Jesus was a high priest after the order of _____.

102. Paul and Silas prayed at what time of day while they were in jail?

_____

103. In what book of the Bible do you find the statement, "Thy navel is like a round goblet"?

_____

104. Who were called, "Liars, evil beasts, slow bellies"?

_____

105. In the book of Luke, who took away the key of knowledge?

_____

106. In what book of the Bible do we find the first mention of a holy kiss?

_____

107. Who sneezed seven times in the Bible?

_____

108. In which book of the Bible do we find the country of Spain mentioned?

_____

109. In what book of the Bible do we find mention of birthing stools?

_____

110. God said that anyone who would kill Cain would receive from Him _____ vengeance.
   a. Threefold   b. Sevenfold   c. Tenfold

111. What were the names of Noah's three daughters-in-law?

_____

112. What was the sign of the covenant between Abram and God?

_____

113. Who said, "Is anything too hard for the Lord?" (NIV)

_____

114. What did Lot offer to the men of the city of Sodom so they would not take the two angels?

_____

115. The division of angels called seraphs (seraphims—KJV) have how many wings?

_____

116. Who was called the king of righteousness in the book of Hebrews?

_____

117. In what book of the Bible does it talk about God giving names to all of the stars?

_____

118. Name the city in which Paul had his hair cut off because of a vow.

_____

119. On the sixth day the children of Israel were to gather how many omers of manna for each person?

_____

120. Who had the first navy mentioned in the Bible?

_____

121. To whom did Jesus say, "Thou gavest me no kiss"?

_____

122. In the book of Proverbs, the virtuous woman clothed her entire family in what color?

_____

123. What was the former name for the town of Bethel?

_____

124. The eighth plague that the Egyptians experienced was the plague of locusts. A strong wind carried the locusts away in which direction?

_____

■ *Hard Trivia Questions*

1. Whose birthday celebration was the first mentioned in the Bible?

   _____

2. In what book of the Bible does it talk about trading a boy for a harlot?

   _____

3. How many men in the Bible were named Judas?

   _____

4. Who received the first kiss that is mentioned in the Bible?

   _____

5. "The men of _____ were wicked and sinners before the Lord exceedingly."

6. In what book of the Bible do we find the first mention of a physician?

   _____

7. When Jeremiah said that all their heads would be shaved and their beards clipped, who was he speaking about?

_____

8. Whose lips quivered and bones decayed when he heard the voice of the Lord?

_____

9. In what book of the Bible do you find the words, "Thine eyes like the fishpools in Heshbon"?

_____

10. Who was the first man the Bible says had a dream?

_____

11. In what book of the Bible do we find God's punishment of "consumption, and the burning ague"?

_____

12. How many chapters are in the book of Esther?

_____

13. How much money did the innkeeper receive from the Good Samaritan for taking care of the sick man?

_____

14. In what book of the Bible do we find the first mention of a "lunatic"?

_____

15. King Solomon had how many horsemen?

_____

16. In what book of the Bible do we have the first mention of magicians?

_____

17. Who does the Bible say eats, wipes her mouth, and says, "I've done nothing wrong"?

_____

18. What did David do with Goliath's weapons?

_____

19. In the end of the book of Job, how many camels did God give to Job?

_____

20. When Elijah built the altar on Mount Carmel, how many stones did he use?

_____

21. What were the names of Pharaoh's two store cities in the book of Exodus?

_____

22. In the book of Ruth, what was Naomi's other name?

_____

23. In what book of the Bible does God say there will be showers of blessing?

_____

24. In which book of the Bible do you read the words, "Be sure your sin will find you out"?

_____

25. Nabal owned how many goats?

_____

26. When Josiah heard God's law read, he did what?

_____

27. In what book of the Bible do we find mention of 20,000 baths of wine and 20,000 baths of oil?

_____

28. In Zechariah's vision of four chariots, what was the color of the horses pulling the fourth chariot?

_____

29. One book in the Bible has the same amount of chapters as there are books in the Bible. What is the name of the book?

_____

30. What was the name of Jonah's father?

_____

31. How many chapters are in the book of Nehemiah?

_____

32. What was the occupation of Shiphrah and Puah?

_____

33. What animal was never to be cooked in its mother's milk?

_____

34. Rahab the harlot hid the two Jewish spies under what?

_____

35. What are the names of the two women who argued over who would get to sleep with their mutual husband?

_____

36. Miriam played what kind of musical instrument?

_____

37. What does the Bible say manna tasted like?

_____

38. What Bible character was called a wild donkey of a man?

_____

39. When King Nebuchadnezzar went crazy, his fingernails began to look like _____.

40. What is the last word in the Bible?

_____

41. What Bible character fell in love with his sister?

_____

42. The prophet Amos tended two things. What were they?

_____

43. The Ark of the Testimony or Covenant was covered with what color cloth when it was moved?

_____

44. Who was the first Bible character mentioned as living in a tent?

_____

45. What is the name of the Bible character who ran faster than a chariot?

_____

46. What three colors were used in sewing the tabernacle curtains?

_____

47. Who came out with bald heads and raw shoulders after a long siege against the city of Tyre?

_____

48. At what time of day did the sailors going to Rome on the ship with Paul first sense land after the storm?

_____

49. In the book of Acts, how many soldiers guarded Peter while he was in prison?

_____

50. Who was the first man in the Bible mentioned as being sick?

_____

51. Who was the fourth oldest man in the Bible?

_____

52. How many yoke of oxen did Job own before tragedy entered his life?

_____

53. In Elim, the Israelites found 70 palm trees and _____ springs (fountains).

54. Moses was told by the Lord to write what on the staff of each leader of the tribes of Israel?

_____

55. Hannah was taunted by_____about not having a baby.

56. Certain Athenian philosophers thought Paul the apostle was a _____.

57. Zechariah had a vision of a basket (ephah). What was in the basket?

_____

58. When King Shishak stole the gold shields from the temple, who replaced them with bronze (brass) shields?

_____

59. In what book of the Bible do we find mention of the name Narcissus?

_____

60. In what book of the Bible do you find the words, "The joy of the Lord is my strength"?

_____

61. Who is the first person in the Bible mentioned as writing a letter?

_____

62. Who received the first letter written in the Bible?

_____

63. Who said, "If I perish, I perish"?

_____

64. Name the shortest book in the Old Testament.
    a. Jonah   b. Nehemiah   c. Obadiah
    d. Zephaniah   e. Malachi

65. The Recabites refused to drink_____.

66. The woman who poured perfume on Jesus' head carried the perfume in what kind of jar?

_____

67. Who does the Bible say was the most humble man?

_____

68. Who was Asenath's famous husband?

_____

69. Who bored a hole in the lid of a chest so that it could become a bank to hold money?

_____

70. After feeding the 4000 men, Jesus went where?

_____

71. What is the name of the prophet who said that Paul would be arrested in Jerusalem?

_____

72. When the temple in the Old Testament was moved, what kind of animal skins were put over the Ark of the Testimony or Covenant?

_____

73. What was the name of the dying king who was propped up in his chariot for a whole day?

_____

74. The Anakites (Anakims—KJV) and the Emites (Emims—KJV) had a common physical characteristic. What was it?

_____

75. King Solomon had his carriage upholstered in what color of material?

_____

76. In which book of the Bible do we find the first mention of the name Satan?

_____

77. The invalid had been lying by the pool of Bethesda for how many years?

_____

78. Mary washed Jesus' feet with what kind of perfume?

_____

79. What did Jacob name the place where he wrestled with a man?

_____

80. When Jacob wrestled with a man, what were the man's first words to Jacob?

_____

81. How many men did Esau bring with him when he came to meet Jacob?
   a. 100   b. 200   c. 300   d. 400   e. 500

82. What special physical feature did Leah have?

_____

83. Elisha was plowing the ground with how many yoke of oxen when Elijah found him?

_____

84. In what book of the Bible does it talk about people who could not tell their right hand from their left hand?

_____

85. What is the name of the man who raped Dinah?

_____

86. When Job became ill, his skin turned to what color?

_____

87. David's delegation to King Hanun had to stay in what town until their beards had grown back?

_____

88. What woman's name is mentioned most often in the Bible?

_____

89. Gideon was the father of how many sons?

_____

90. What is the name of the king who had 900 iron chariots?

_____

91. King Solomon had how many steps to his throne?

_____

92. What was the name of Isaiah's father?

_____

93. David was betrothed to Saul's daughter for how many Philistine foreskins?

_____

94. After the Philistines cut off Saul's head, they put it in the temple of _____.

95. Deborah, the Old Testament judge, sat under what kind of tree?

_____

96. In the parable of the Good Samaritan, who was the second person to ignore the injured man?

_____

97. When King Ben-Hadad attacked Samaria, how many kings helped him?

_____

98. Jonathan, Ishvi, and Malki-Shua had a famous father. What was his name?

_____

99. What is the name of the Bible prophet who was lifted by his hair between heaven and earth to see a vision?

_____

100. What name did Amos call the sinful women of Israel?

_____

101. Nehemiah went to the keeper of the king's forest to get wood. What was the forest-keeper's name?

_____

102. When is the first time love is mentioned in the Bible?

_____

103. In which book of the Bible do we find the only mention of the name Lucifer?

_____

104. What Bible character said, "By my God have I leaped over a wall"?

_____

105. Who was the first left-handed man mentioned in the Bible?

_____

106. Who called Israel a "backsliding heifer"?

_____

107. Who said, "Man is born into trouble, as the sparks fly upward"?

_____

108. The river Pishon flowed out of the Garden of Eden into the land of _____, where there was gold.

109. In what book of the Bible do we find mention of the word stargazers?

    _____

110. The name "Ziz" was _____.
    a. A city   b. A brook   c. A cliff   d. A soldier
    e. A priest   f. None of the above

111. Jazer was _____.
    a. A king   b. A land   c. A priest   d. A river
    e. A servant f. None of the above

112. How old was Adam when he died?

    _____

113. Who was the father of Enoch?

    _____

114. How many days after the tops of the mountains appeared did Noah wait before he opened the window of the Ark?

    _____

115. Who was the famous son of Terah?

    _____

116. When Lot left Sodom, what city did he flee to?

    _____

117. What are the names of the two children who were born to Lot's two daughters?

    _____

118. How old was Sarah when she died?
    a. 103   b. 112   c. 127   d. 133

119. What were the names of the two wives of Esau who caused Isaac and Rebekah much grief?

    _____

120. Who was the second oldest man in the Bible?

_____

121. How old was Enoch when God took him to heaven?

_____

122. The Israelites hung their harps on what kind of trees?

_____

123. After baptizing the eunuch, Philip was taken by the Spirit of the Lord to what city?

_____

124. How long did Job live after the Lord made him prosperous again?

_____

125. What was the name of Eli's grandson?

_____

■ *Trivia Questions For the Expert*

1. Who were the men of whom God said, "Thou shalt make for them girdles, and bonnets"?

   _____

2. Which book in the Bible talks about men who "belch out with their mouth"?

   _____

3. In what book of the Bible does it talk about ice coming out of the womb?

   _____

4. Who laughed when threatened with a spear?

   _____

5. In what book of the Bible do we find mention of "wimples and the crisping pins"?

   _____

6. What is the name of the Bible character who had 30 sons who rode on 30 donkeys and controlled 30 cities?

   _____

7. In what book of the Bible do we have the first mention of a barber's razor?

_____

8. The angel of the Lord killed how many of Sennacherib's soldiers?

_____

9. How many times is the Old Testament quoted in the book of Revelation?

_____

10. In what verse of the Bible do we find the word "cankerworm" mentioned twice?

_____

11. In what book of the Bible do we find the only two occurrences of the word rainbow?

_____

12. In what book of the Bible do we read the words, "Twisting the nose produces blood" (NIV)?

_____

13. What is the name of the Bible character who said, "I have escaped with only the skin of my teeth" (NIV)?

_____

14. According to King Solomon, good news gives health to what part of our body?

_____

15. How long did Ezekiel lie on his right side for the sins of Judah?

_____

16. What book of the Bible talks about "five gold tumors and five gold rats" (NIV)?

_____

17. The bronze snake that Moses made was broken into pieces by what king?

18. What Bible character was smothered to death by a wet cloth?

19. Which chapter in the book of Psalms could be a statement against abortion?

20. What book of the Bible talks about a man "that hath a flat nose"?

21. What Bible character was known for his threats to gouge out the right eye of the people who lived in Jabesh Gilead?

22. How close to the city of Jericho was the brook of Ziba?

23. Who was the high priest when Nehemiah rebuilt the walls of Jerusalem?

24. How many men did Solomon use to cut stone for the temple?

25. The Bible says that what bird is cruel to her young?

26. God spoke to Jeremiah and said something that is a good argument against abortion. What was that statement?

27. What was the name of Ezekiel's father?

28. What Bible character thought laughter was a foolish thing?

_____

29. In what book of the Bible do you find the first mention of using battering rams against gates of a city?

_____

30. God showed a basket to the prophet Amos. What was in that basket?

_____

31. The word eternity is used _____ times in the Bible.

32. Ahab's 70 sons had their heads cut off and sent in baskets to what man?

_____

33. Which Bible character had the first king-sized bed?

_____

34. In which two books of the Bible do we read about cannibalism?

_____

35. Which family in the Bible did not have to pay taxes?

_____

36. The Bible says that storks build their nests in what kind of trees?

_____

37. How did God destroy the kings who attacked Gibeon?

_____

38. In what book of the Bible does it talk about nose jewelry?

_____

39. What Bible character had his thumbs and big toes cut off by the tribes of Judah and Simeon?

_____

40. What Bible character hid his belt (girdle—KJV) in the crevice of the rocks?

_____

41. What is the name of the young virgin who kept King David warm during his old age?

_____

42. King Saul sat under what kind of tree while Jonathan went to attack the Philistines?

_____

43. What was the name of Abraham's servant?

_____

44. How many chapters are there in the entire Bible?

_____

45. Who was the father of Ziddim, Zer, Hammath, Rakkath, and Kinnereth?

_____

46. How many chapters are there in the Old Testament?

_____

47. What Bible character was beheaded, cremated, and then buried?

_____

48. In what book of the Bible do we find mention of "mufflers"?

_____

49. Gideon received golden earrings as payment for conquering the Midianites. How much did the earrings weigh?

_____

50. What is the most used word in the Bible?

_____

51. The valley of Siddim was famous for what?

_____

52. Where was Ishbosheth's head buried?

_____

53. When the tabernacle was built, who was the chief crafts-
    man?

_____

54. What emotion will cause your bones to rot?

_____

55. What group of people were told to burn their hair after
    it was cut off?

_____

56. Who was told to say, "My little finger is thicker than
    my father's waist" (NIV)?

_____

57. In what book of the Bible do you find the "hill of the
    foreskins"?

_____

58. Hezekiah had a poultice put on his boil. What was the
    poultice made of?

_____

59. What was the name of Goliath's brother?

_____

60. What three things did the Pharisees and scribes tithe?

_____

61. What are the names of the two women who had their ages
    recorded in the Bible?

_____

62. What was the name of the eunuch who was in charge of King Xerxes' (King Ahasuerus—KJV) concubines?

_____

63. What Bible character is mentioned as having an incurable bowel disease?

_____

64. What Bible character said that soldiers should be content with their pay?

_____

65. The horses of the Babylonians (Chaldeans—KJV) were likened to what kind of animals?
    a. Lions b. Leopards c. Deer d. Sheep e. Eagles

66. What did Moses throw into the air to signal the start of the plague of boils on Egypt?

_____

67. In what book of the Bible do we find mention of "round tires like the moon"?

_____

68. In Zechariah's vision, the man on the red horse was riding among what kind of trees?

_____

69. What is the name of the man who tried to humiliate David's army by cutting off half of each soldier's beard and their garments in the middle at the buttocks?

_____

70. What is the name of the man who wrote Proverbs 30?

_____

71. In the book of Revelation, Antipas was martyred in
    _____ for his faith.

72. How many Bible characters are mentioned as living over 900 years?
    a. 3   b. 5   c. 7   d. 9   e. 11

73. Solomon made the steps of the temple and the palace out of what kind of wood?

    _____

74. What were the first words Elisha spoke when he saw Elijah going to heaven?

    _____

75. How many suicides are mentioned in the Bible?

    _____

76. The wicked King Abimelech was critically injured by a woman dropping a_____on his head.

77. How many days was Ezekiel told to lie on his side while eating only bread and water?

    _____

78. King Asa had what kind of disease?

    _____

79. God punished David for taking a census of the people. How many people died in God's punishment?

    _____

80. The Israelites were told not to destroy what when they besieged cities in the Old Testament?

    _____

81. How many shekels of silver did Achan steal?

    _____

82. The name Judas Iscariot appears how many times in the Bible?

    _____

83. When Rachel stole some household gods from her father, she hid them in a camel's saddle and sat on the saddle. When her father came looking for the images, what excuse did Rachel use for not getting off the camel's saddle?

_____

84. Obadiah hid _____ prophets in caves to protect them from Jezebel.

85. When the tower of Siloam fell, how many people were killed?

_____

86. What Bible character talks about beautiful feet?

_____

87. In what book of the Bible does it say, "Our skin was black like an oven because of the terrible famine"?

_____

88. In what book of the Bible do we find the famous verse, "At Parbar westward, four at the causeway, and two at Parbar"?

_____

89. What Bible character cooked his bread on cow dung?

_____

90. Name the only book in the Bible that is addressed specifically to a woman.

_____

91. How many people were shipwrecked with the apostle Paul in the book of Acts?

_____

92. Who was the famous father of Maher-Shalel-Hash-Baz?

_____

93. What is the name of the king of Judah who made war machines that could shoot arrows and hurl huge stones?

94. What was the name of Haman's wife?

95. How many times does the name Satan appear in the Bible?

96. The manna in the wilderness was likened to what kind of seed?

97. What will bring "health to thy navel and marrow to thy bones"?

98. Which town in the Bible had silver heaped up like dust and fine gold like the dirt of the streets?

99. In what book of the Bible do we have mention of "sea monsters"?

100. How many times is the word Lord mentioned in the Bible?
     a. 5,017   b. 6,370   c. 7,736   d. 8,212   e. 9,108

101. In what two books of the Bible does it talk about men drinking their own urine and eating their own refuse?

102. Which book of the Bible mentions men "fearing lest they should fall into the quicksands"?

103. To whom did Ebed-melech, the Ethiopian say, "Put now these . . . rotten rags under thine armholes"?

104. What man in the Bible did not shave or wash his clothes for many days?

105. Who grabbed Amasa by the beard with his right hand and pretended that he was going to kiss him, but instead stabbed him with a dagger?

106. How many times is Beer mentioned in the Bible?

107. In what book of the Bible do we have the only mention of a ferry boat?

108. What two tribes built an altar between them and called it Ed?

109. Where in the Bible does it talk about a gathering of the sheriffs?

110. In which book of the Bible does it talk about melting slugs or snails?

111. How many times is the word "the" used in the Bible?
     a. Over 9,000   b. Over 11,000   c. Over 14,000
     d. Over 20,000

112. In what book of the Bible do we find mention of stars singing?

113. How many times is the word suburbs mentioned in the Bible?

_____

114. How many times are unicorns mentioned in the Bible?

_____

115. Who was the brother of Zered?

_____

116. If Cain was to be avenged sevenfold, how many times would Lamech be avenged?

_____

117. To how many people did God say, "Be fruitful, and multiply, and replenish the earth"?

_____

118. What time of day did God rain down fire and brimstone on Sodom and Gomorrah?

_____

119. What did Abraham call the name of the place where he was about to sacrifice Isaac?

_____

120. How old was Esau when he married his two wives Judith and Basemath?

_____

121. Isaiah prophesied that_____women would take hold of one man.

122. Zechariah saw a vision of a scroll that was _____ feet long.

123. Who was the first man to say, "I have sinned" in the Bible?

_____

124. The Bible character Zaphenath-Paneah was known by another famous name. What was that name?

_____

125. In Zechariah's vision, the flying scroll was how wide?

_____

■ Puns, Riddles, and Humorous Trivia Questions

1. On the Ark, Noah probably got milk from the cows. What did he get from the ducks?

   _____

2. One of the first things Cain did after he left the Garden of Eden was to take a nap. How do we know this?

   _____

3. Where do you think the Israelites may have deposited their money?

   _____

4. Why do you think that the kangaroo was the most miserable animal on the Ark?

   _____

5. What prophet in the Bible was a space traveler?

   _____

6. What do you have that Cain, Abel, and Seth never had?

   _____

7. What city in the Bible was named after something that you find on every modern-day car?

_____

8. When the Ark landed on Mount Ararat, was Noah the first one out?

_____

9. What was the difference between the 10,000 soldiers of Israel and the 300 soldiers Gideon chose for battle?

_____

10. Where is the first math problem mentioned in the Bible?

_____

11. Where is the second math problem mentioned in the Bible?

_____

12. Why did Noah have to punish and discipline the chickens on the Ark?

_____

13. What was the most expensive meal served in the Bible and who ate it?

_____

14. Certain days in the Bible passed by more quickly than most of the days. Which days were these?

_____

15. Matthew and Mark have something that is not found in Luke and John. What is it?

_____

16. Which one of Noah's sons was considered to be a clown?

_____

17. What was the first game mentioned in the Bible?

_____

18. What made Abraham so smart?

_____

19. What is most of the time black, sometimes brown or
    white, but should be red?

_____

20. Why did everyone on the Ark think that the horses were
    pessimistic?

_____

21. Who was the first person in the Bible to have surgery
    performed on him?

_____

22. When was the Red Sea very angry?

_____

23. What vegetable did Noah not want on the Ark?

_____

24. Why do you think Jonah could not trust the ocean?

_____

25. How do we know that God has a sense of humor?

_____

26. What time was it when the hippopotamus sat on Noah's
    rocking chair?

_____

27. What does God both give away and keep at the same
    time?

_____

28. During the six days of creation, which weighed more—the
    day or the night?

_____

29. What did the skunks on the Ark have that no other animals had?

_____

30. What type of tea does the Bible suggest that we not drink?

_____

31. In what book of the Bible do we find something that is in modern-day courtrooms?

_____

32. Which animal on the Ark was the rudest?

_____

33. What kind of soap did God use to keep the oceans clean?

_____

34. How do we know that the disciples were very cruel to the corn?

_____

35. Why did the rooster refuse to fight on the Ark?

_____

36. Why didn't Cain please the Lord with his offering?

_____

37. One of the names of the books of the Bible contains an insect in it. Which one is it?

_____

38. How many animals could Noah put into the empty Ark?

_____

39. Which man in the Bible might have only been 12 inches?

_____

40. Which book in the Bible is the counting book?

_____

41. What kind of lights did Noah have on the Ark?

_____

42. Gideon had 70 sons. How many of them were big men when they were born?

_____

43. Which candle burns longer—the candle hidden under a bushel or the candle set on a hill?

_____

44. Which animal on Noah's Ark had the highest level of intelligence?

_____

45. What indication is there that there may have been newspaper reporters in the New Testament?

_____

46. The name of one book of the Bible contains an ugly old woman. Which book is it?

_____

47. Which animal on the Ark did Noah not trust?

_____

48. Which Bible character was as strong as steel?

_____

49. What man in the Bible is named after a chicken?

_____

50. Where does the Bible suggest that it is okay to be overweight?

_____

51. What Bible character had a name that rang a bell?

_____

52. Which bird on Noah's Ark was a thief?

_____

53. Where does the Bible suggest that newspapers, magazines, radio, and television are powerful?

_____

54. What is the name of the individual who was perfect in the Bible?

_____

55. What was Eve's formal name?

_____

56. On Noah's Ark, why did the dog have so many friends?

_____

57. Who killed a fourth of all the people in the world?

_____

58. Where does it suggest that there may have been buses in the Bible?

_____

59. When Eve left the garden without Adam, what did Adam say?

_____

60. When a camel with no hump was born on the Ark, what did Noah name it?

_____

61. How long did Samson love Delilah?

_____

62. Where were freeways first mentioned in the Bible?

_____

63. What is the name of the sleepiest land in the Bible?

_____

64. What did Noah call the cat that fell into the pickle barrel on the Ark?

_____

65. What age were the goats when Adam named them in the Garden of Eden?

_____

66. David played a dishonest musical instrument. What was it called?

_____

67. Which of the Old Testament prophets were blind?

_____

68. How did Noah keep the milk from turning sour on the Ark?

_____

69. How many books in the Old Testament were named after Esther?

_____

70. What would have happened if all the women would have left the nation of Israel?

_____

71. Why did the giant fish finally let Jonah go?

_____

72. Why was Moses buried in a valley in the land of Moab near Bethpeor?

_____

73. The name of a book of the Bible contains a fruit. Which book is it?

_____

74. What is in the wall of Jerusalem that the Israelites did not put there?

_____

75. Why was "W" the nastiest letter in the Bible?

_____

76. How did Joseph learn to tell the naked truth?

_____

77. What food did Samson eat to become strong?

_____

78. Why did the tower of Babel stand in the land of Shinar?

_____

79. Why did Moses have to be hidden quickly when he was a baby?

_____

80. Where in the Bible do we find the authority for women to kiss men?

_____

81. What two things could Samson the Nazarite never eat for breakfast?

_____

82. If Elijah was invited to dinner and was served only a beet, what would he say?

_____

83. If a man crosses the Sea of Galilee twice without a bath, what would he be?

_____

84. If someone wanted to be converted by John the Baptist, what was the first requirement?

_____

85. What day of the week was the best for cooking manna in the wilderness?

_____

86. If a soft answer turneth away wrath, what does a hard answer do?

_____

87. In what book of the Bible does it talk about people wearing tires on their heads?

_____

88. What is the golden rule of the animal world?

_____

89. How did Adam and Eve feel when they left the garden?

_____

90. Samson was a very strong man but there was one thing he could not hold for very long. What was that?

_____

91. If Moses would have dropped his rod in the Red Sea, what would it have become?

_____

92. What fur did Adam and Eve wear?

_____

93. Why must Elijah's parents have been good business people?

_____

94. Jesus and the giant fish that swallowed Jonah have something in common. What is it?

_____

95. What did Joseph in the Old Testament have in common with Zaccheus in the New Testament?

_____

96. In what way does an attorney resemble a rabbi?

_____

97. What does a Christian man love more than life;
    Hate more than death or mortal strife;
    That which contented men desire;
    The poor have, the rich require;
    The miser spends, the spendthrift saves;
    And all men carry to their graves?

_____

98. What is that which Adam never saw or possessed, yet
    left two for each of his children?

_____

99. What is greater than God, not as wicked as Satan,
    if people are alive and eat it they will die, and dead
    people eat it?

_____

■ *Melody in F*
(The Prodigal Son)

Feeling footloose and frisky, a featherbrained
    fellow
Forced his fond father to fork over the
    farthings.
And flew far to foreign fields
And frittered his fortune feasting
    fabulously with faithless friends.

Fleeced by his fellows in folly, and facing
    famine,
He found himself a feed-flinger in a filthy
    farmyard.
Fairly famishing, he fain would have filled
    his frame
With foraged food from fodder
    fragments.

"Fooey, my father's flunkies fare far
    finer,"
The frazzled fugitive forlornly fumbled,
    frankly facing facts.

Frustrated by failure, and filled with
    foreboding,
He fled forthwith to his family.
Falling at his father's feet, he forlornly
    fumbled,
"Father, I've flunked,
And fruitlessly forfeited family fellowship
    favor."

The farsighted father, forestalling further
    flinching,
Frantically flagged the flunkies to
Fetch a fatling from the flock and fix a
    feast.
The fugitive's faultfinding brother
    frowned
On fickle forgiveness of former folderol.

But the faithful father figured,
"Filial fidelity is fine, but the fugitive is
    found!
What forbids fervent festivity?
Let flags be unfurled! Let fanfares flare!"
Father's forgiveness formed the
    foundation
For the former fugitive's future fortitude!

■ *The Christ*
Of the Bible

More than 1900 years ago there was a Man born contrary to the laws of life. This Man lived in poverty and was reared in obscurity. He did not travel extensively. Only once did He cross the boundary of the country in which He lived and that was during His exile in childhood.

He possessed neither name, wealth, nor influence. His relatives were inconspicuous, uninfluential, and had neither training nor education.

In infancy He startled a king; in childhood He puzzled the doctors; in manhood He ruled the course of nature, walked upon billows as if pavements, and hushed the sea to sleep.

He healed the multitudes without medicine and made no charge for His service.

He never wrote a book, and yet all the libraries of the country could not hold the books that have been written about Him.

He never wrote a song, and yet He has furnished the theme for more songs than all the songwriters combined.

He never founded a college, but all the schools put together cannot boast of having as many students.

He never practiced medicine, and yet He has healed more broken hearts than all the doctors far and near.

He never marshalled an army, nor drafted a soldier, nor fired a gun, and yet no leader ever had more volunteers who have, under His orders, made more rebels stack arms and surrender without a shot being fired.

He is the Star of astronomy, the Rock of geology, the Lion and Lamb of the zoological kingdom.

He is the Revealer of the snares that lurk in the darkness; the Rebuker of every evil thing that prowls by night; the Quickener of all that is wholesome; the Adorner of all that is beautiful; the Reconciler of all that is contradictory; the Harmonizer of all discords; the Healer of all diseases; and the Savior of all mankind.

He fills the pages of theology and hymnology. Every prayer that goes up to God goes up in His name and is asked to be granted for His sake.

Every seventh day the wheels of commerce cease their turning and multitudes wend their way to worshiping assemblies to pay homage and respect to Him.

The names of the past proud statesmen of Greece and Rome have come and gone. The names of the past scientists, philosophers, and theologians have come and gone; but the name of this Man abounds more and more. Though time has spread 1900 years between the people of this generation and the scene of His crucifixion, yet He still lives. Herod could not kill Him. Satan could not seduce Him. Death could not hold Him.

He stands forth upon the highest pinnacle of heavenly glory, proclaimed of God, acknowledged by angels, adored by saints, and feared by devils, as the living, personal Christ.

This Man, as you know, is Jesus Christ, our Lord and Savior!

A study of the Bible reveals Christ as its central subject and great theme. What the hub is to the wheel, Christ is to the Bible. It revolves around Him. All its types point to Him, all its truths converge in Him, all its glories reflect Him, all its promises radiate from Him, all its beauties are embodied by Him, all its demands are exemplified by Him, and all its predictions are accepted by Him.

Abel's lamb was a type of Christ. Abraham offering Isaac on Mount Moriah was a type of God giving Christ, His only Son, on Mount Calvary. The Passover lamb in Egypt was a type of Christ. The brazen serpent in the wilderness was a type of Christ—He told Nicodemus so Himself. The scapegoat typified Him bearing our sins. The scarlet thread that the harlot Rahab hung in the window of her home in Jericho typified Him. Joseph, pictured to us by the Bible without a flaw, was a type of Christ. "Who did not sin, neither was guile found in his mouth."

In the Old Testament He is spoken of as "the angel of the Lord," and as such He appeared unto men.

He was with Adam and Eve in the Garden of Eden. He was with Abel in his death. He walked with Enoch. He rode with Noah in the Ark. He ate with Abraham in his desert tent. He pled with Lot to leave wicked Sodom.

He watched Isaac reopen the wells that his father Abraham had dug. He wrestled with Jacob at Peniel. He strengthened Joseph in his time of temptation, protected him in prison, and exalted him to first place in the kingdom. He watched over Moses in the ark of bulrushes, talked to him from the burning bush, went down into Egypt with him, opened the Red Sea for him, fed him on bread from heaven, protected him with a pillar of fire by night, and after 120 years of such blessed companionship that they left no marks of passing time upon Moses, led him up from the plains of Moab unto the mountain of Nebo, to the top of Pisgah, let him take one long, loving look at the Promised Land, and then kissed him to sleep, folded Moses' hands over his breast, and buried his body in an unmarked grave, to sleep in Jesus till the morning of the great resurrection day.

He was the Captain of the Lord's host to Joshua, led him over the swollen stream of Jordan in flood tide, around Jericho, in conquest of Ai, helped him conquer Canaan, divide the land, and say good-bye to the children of Israel. He was with Gideon and his famous 300. He was with Samuel when he rebuked Saul. He was with David when he wrote the twenty-third psalm. He was with Solomon when he built the first temple. He was with good king Hezekiah when Sennacherib invaded the land. He was with Josiah in his great reformation that brought the people back to the law. He was with Ezekiel and Daniel in Babylon. He was with Jeremiah in Egypt. He was with Ezra when he returned from Babylon, and with Nehemiah when he rebuilt the wall. In fact, He was with all those "who through faith subdued kingdoms, wrought righteousness, obtained promises, stopped the mouths of lions, quenched the violence of fire, escaped the edge of the sword, out of weakness were made strong, waxed valiant in fight, turned to flight the armies of the aliens."

Abraham saw His day and rejoiced. Jacob called Him the "Lawgiver of Judah." Moses called Him the "Prophet that was to come." Job called Him "My Living Redeemer." Daniel called Him the "Ancient of Days." Jeremiah called Him "The Lord our Righteousness." Isaiah called Him "Wonderful Counselor, the Mighty God, the Everlasting Father, the Prince of Peace."

All of this in the Old Testament? Yes, and much more besides. "To Him give all the prophets witness." Micah tells of the place of His birth. Jonah tells of His death, burial, and resurrection. Amos tells of His second coming to build again the tabernacles of David. Joel describes the day of His wrath. Zechariah tells of His coming reign as King over all the earth. Ezekiel gives us a picture of His millennial temple.

In fact, my friends, it matters little where we wander down the aisles, avenues, byways, or highways of the Old Testament. Jesus walks beside us as He walked beside the two disciples on that dusty road to Emmaus on that glorious resurrection day long, long ago.

Its types tell of Him, its sacrifices show Him, its symbols signify Him, its histories are His-stories, its songs are His sentiments, its prophecies are His pictures, its promises are His pledges; and our hearts burn within us as we walk beside Him across its living pages!

When we open the New Testament, the Word which was in the beginning with God becomes flesh and dwells among us, and we behold His glory, the glory as of the only begotten of the Father, full of grace and truth.

There are four personal histories of His earthly life written in the New Testament. One is by Matthew, the redeemed publican, and signifies His lineage; one is by Mark, the unknown servant, which magnifies His service; one is by Luke, "the beloved physician," and tells of His humanity; and one is by John, "whom Jesus loved," and it tells of His deity. He is Christ the King in Matthew, the Servant in Mark, the Man in Luke, and the Incarnate Word in John.

Concerning His royal lineage we learn that He was born in Bethlehem, the Seed of Abraham, the Son of David, the Son of Mary, the Son of God; and was acknowledged as "King of the Jews," "Christ the Lord," "God's Son," "The Savior of Men," by angels, demons, shepherds, and wise men; and that He received tribute of gold, frankincense, and myrrh.

Concerning His service we learn that He labored as a carpenter, opened eyes of the blind, unstopped deaf ears, loosed dumb tongues, cleansed lepers, healed the sick, restored withered hands, fed the hungry, sympathized with the sad, washed the disciples' feet, wept with Mary and Martha, preached the Gospel to the poor, went about doing good, and gave His life as a ransom for many.

Concerning His humanity we learn that He was born of a woman, as a little babe was wrapped in swaddling clothes, grew up and developed as a child in wisdom, stature, and in favor with God and men. He worked with His hands, He grew weary, He hungered, He thirsted, He slept, He felt the surge of anger; knew what it was to be sad, shed tears, sweat drops of blood; was betrayed, went through the mockery of a criminal trial, was scourged, had His hands and feet pierced; wore a crown of thorns, was spit upon, was crucified, was wrapped in a winding sheet, and was buried in a borrowed tomb behind a sealed stone, and was guarded by Roman soldiers in His death.

Concerning His deity we read that He was born of a virgin, lived a sinless life, spoke matchless words, stilled storms, calmed waves, rebuked winds, multiplied loaves, turned water to wine, raised the dead, foretold the future, gave hearing to the deaf, sight to the blind, speech to the dumb, cast out demons, healed diseases, forgave sins, claimed equality with God, arose from the dead, possessed all authority both in heaven and in earth.

He was both God and Man; two individuals united in one personality. "As a man, He thirsted; as God, He gave living water. As a man, He went to a wedding; as God, He turned the water to wine. As man, He slept in a boat; as God, He stilled the storm. As man, He was tempted; as God, He sinned not. As man, He wept; as God, He raised Lazarus from the dead. As man, He prayed; as God, He makes intercession for all men."

This is what Paul means when he writes, "Without controversy great is the mystery of godliness; God was manifest in the flesh, justified in the Spirit, seen of angels, preached unto the Gentiles, believed on in the world, received up into glory." He was made unto us wisdom, righteousness, sanctification, and redemption. He is the Light of this world. He is the Bread of Life. He is the True Vine. He is the Good Shepherd. He is the Way. He is the Life. He is the Door to Heaven.

He is the Faithful Witness, the First Begotten of the dead, the Prince of the kings of the earth, the King of Kings, and the Lord of lords, Alpha and Omega, the first and the last, the beginning and the ending, the Lord who is, who was, and who is to come, the Almighty. "I am He that liveth, and was dead; and behold, I am alive forevermore, and I have the keys of hell and of death."

He is the theme of the Bible from beginning to end: He is my Savior, let Him be your Savior, too!

    In Genesis He is the Seed of the Woman
    In Exodus He is the Passover Lamb
    In Leviticus He is our High Priest
    In Numbers He is the Pillar of Cloud by day and the Pillar of Fire by night
    In Deuteronomy He is the Prophet like unto Moses
    In Joshua He is the Captain of our Salvation
    In Judges He is our Judge and Lawgiver

In Ruth He is our Kinsman Redeemer

In 1 and 2 Samuel He is our Trusted Prophet

In Kings and Chronicles He is our Reigning King

In Ezra He is the Rebuilder of the broken-down walls of human life

In Esther He is our Mordecai

And in Job He is our Ever-Living Redeemer, "For I know my redeemer liveth."

In Psalms He is our Shepherd

In Proverbs and Ecclesiastes He is our Wisdom

In the Song of Solomon He is our Lover and Bridegroom

In Isaiah He is the Prince of Peace

In Jeremiah He is the Righteous Branch

In Lamentations He is our Weeping Prophet

In Ezekiel He is the wonderful Four-Faced Man

And in Daniel the Fourth Man in "Life's Fiery Furnaces."

In Hosea He is the Faithful Husband, "Forever married to the backslider."

In Joel He is the Baptizer with the Holy Ghost and Fire

In Amos He is our Burden-Bearer

In Obadiah He is the Mighty to Save

In Jonah He is our great Foreign Missionary

In Micah He is the Messenger of Beautiful Feet

In Nahum He is the Avenger of God's Elect

In Habakkuk He is God's Evangelist, crying, "Revive thy work in the midst of the years."

In Zephaniah He is our Savior

In Haggai He is the Restorer of God's lost heritage

In Zechariah He is the Fountain opened to the house of David for sin and uncleanness

In Malachi He is the Sun of Righteousness, rising with healing in His wings

In Matthew He is the Messiah

In Mark He is the Wonder-Worker

In Luke He is the Son of Man

In John He is the Son of God

In Acts He is the Holy Ghost

In Romans He is our Justifier
In 1 and 2 Corinthians He is our Sanctifier
In Galatians He is our Redeemer from the curse of the
    law
In Ephesians He is the Christ of unsearchable riches
In Philippians He is the God who supplies all our needs
In Colossians He is the fullness of the Godhead, bodily
In 1 and 2 Thessalonians He is our Soon-Coming King
In 1 and 2 Timothy He is our Mediator between God and
    man
In Titus He is our Faithful Pastor
In Philemon He is a Friend that sticketh closer than a
    brother
In Hebrews He is the Blood of the Everlasting Covenant
In James He is our Great Physician, for "The prayer
    of faith shall save the sick."
In 1 and 2 Peter He is our Chief Shepherd, who soon shall
    appear with a crown of unfading glory
In 1, 2, and 3 John He is Love
In Jude He is the Lord coming with ten thousands of
    His saints
And in Revelation He is the King of kings and Lord of
    lords!

He is Abel's Sacrifice, Noah's Rainbow, Abraham's Ram,
Isaac's Wells, Jacob's Ladder, Issachar's Burdens, Jacob's
Sceptre, Balaam's Shiloh, Moses' Rod, Joshua's Sun and Moon
that stood still, Elijah's Mantle, Elisha's Staff, Gideon's Fleece,
Samuel's Horn of Oil, David's Slingshot, Isaiah's Fig Poultice,
Hezekiah's Sundial, Daniel's Visions, Amos' Burden, and
Malachi's Sun of Righteousness.

He is Peter's Shadow, Stephen's Signs and Wonders, Paul's
Handkerchiefs and Aprons, and John's Pearly White City.

He is a Father to the Orphan, Husband to the Widow, to the
traveler in the night He is the Bright and Morning Star, to those
who walk in the Lonesome Valley He is the Lily of the Valley,
the Rose of Sharon, and Honey in the Rock.

He is the Brightness of God's Glory, the Express Image of His Person, the King of Glory, the Pearl of Great Price, the Rock in a Weary Land, the Cup that runneth over, the Rod and Staff that comfort, and the Government of our life is upon His shoulders.

He is Jesus of Nazareth, the Son of the living God! My Savior, my Companion, my Lord and King!

—Author unknown

■ *Answers to Easy Trivia Questions*

1. What was the name of the garden Jesus prayed in?
   A: Gethsemane—Matthew 26:36
2. In what book of the Bible do we read about God's armor?
   A: Ephesians 6
3. "Without the _____ _____ _____ there is no forgiveness" (NIV).
   A: Shedding of blood—Hebrews 9:22
4. How many demons did Mary Magdalene have in her?
   a. Two   b. Three   c. Five   d. Seven   e. Nine
   A: "D" or seven—Luke 8:2
5. How old was the daughter of Jairus?
   A: About 12—Luke 8:42
6. What book comes before 1 Kings?
   A: 2 Samuel
7. What are the names of the two men who had a sharp argument over John Mark?
   A: Paul and Barnabas—Acts 15:39
8. Which chapter in the Bible lists the heroes of faith?
   A: Hebrews 11

9. What Bible character stood on Mars Hill?
   A: Paul—Acts 17:22

10. "With God all things are _____."
    A: Possible—Matthew 19:26

11. A man who has his quiver full of them is happy. What is in the quiver?
    A: Children (KJV); sons (NIV)—Psalm 127:4,5

12. Who was the first person to experience fear in the Bible?
    A: Adam—Genesis 3:9,10

13. " _____ _____ is the same yesterday and today and forever" (NIV).
    A: Jesus Christ—Hebrews 13:8

14. Peter says that in the last days_____will come.
    A: Scoffers—2 Peter 3:3

15. Who shut the door on Noah's Ark?
    A: The Lord—Genesis 7:16

16. What time of day did Adam and Eve hear God walking in the Garden of Eden?
    A: In the cool of the day—Genesis 3:8

17. Who said, "I will exalt my throne above the stars of God"?
    A: Lucifer—Isaiah 14:13

18. What Bible character talks about "the twinkling of an eye"?
    A: Paul—1 Corinthians 15:52; 1:1,2

19. Who was the first person in the Bible to take a nap?
    A: Adam—Genesis 2:20,21

20. Paul prayed _____ times to have his thorn in the flesh removed.
    A: Three—2 Corinthians 12:7,8

21. Quote Romans 3:23.
    A: "For all have sinned, and come short of the glory of God."

22. What Bible character said, "Where your treasure is, there will your heart be also"?
    A: Jesus—Luke 12:34

23. What is the book just before Micah?
    A: Jonah

24. Into how many pieces was Jesus' seamless garment cut?
    A: It was not cut—John 19:23,24
25. In what book of the Bible does it talk about 100-pound (or a talent) hailstones?
    A: Revelation—Revelation 16:21
26. Who had a spear with the iron head weighing 600 shekels?
    A: Goliath—1 Samuel 17:4,7
27. In what chapter of the Bible do we find Jesus' high priestly prayer?
    A: John 17
28. The Egyptians thought Sarah was related to Abraham in what way?
    A: They thought she was his sister—Genesis 12:19
29. Which tribe of Israel had the responsibility of moving the tabernacle?
    A: Levi—Numbers 1:51
30. What book comes after the book of Obadiah?
    A: Jonah
31. What is the first word in the Bible?
    A: In—Genesis 1:1
32. In what chapter of the Bible do you find the phrase, "He leadeth me beside the still waters"?
    A: Psalm 23—Psalm 23:2
33. God told Adam and Eve not to eat what kind of fruit?
    A: The Bible does not say.
34. "_____ goeth before destruction, and a haughty spirit before a fall."
    A: Pride—Proverbs 16:18
35. When Jesus was 12 He was unintentionally left behind by Mary and Joseph. How many days did they look for Him?
    A: Three—Luke 2:46
36. How many times a year did the high priest enter the Holy of Holies to make atonement for all the sins of Israel?
    A: Once a year—Leviticus 16:34
37. Who said, "Naked I came from my mother's womb" (NIV)?
    A: Job—Job 1:21,22

38. How old was Jesus when it was first mentioned that He went to Jerusalem for the Passover?
    A: Twelve—Luke 2:42
39. How many men believed in Christ after Peter's second sermon?
    A: About 5000—Acts 4:4
40. "For the wages of sin is _____, but the gift of God is _____ _____" (NIV).
    A: Death, eternal life—Romans 6:23
41. Two Old Testament cities were destroyed because of their great wickedness. What were their names?
    A: Sodom and Gomorrah—Genesis 19:28,29
42. In the Garden of Gethsemane, Jesus sweat great drops of _____.
    A: Blood—Luke 22:44
43. The Bible suggests that a thousand years in God's sight is as how long?
    A: A day—Psalm 90:4
44. Who said, "Foxes have holes and birds of the air have nests" (NIV)?
    A: Jesus—Matthew 8:20
45. Which of the 12 disciples was in charge of the money?
    A: Judas Iscariot—John 12:4-6
46. What book comes before the book of Lamentations?
    A: Jeremiah
47. Who said, "Before Abraham was born, I am" (NIV)?
    A: Jesus—John 8:58
48. In what book of the Bible do we find the quotation, "God helps those who help themselves"?
    A: It is not in the Bible.
49. What is the name of the disciple who took care of Jesus' mother after His death?
    A: John, the disciple whom Jesus loved—John 19:26,27
50. Quote Philippians 4:4.
    A: "Rejoice in the Lord always. I will say it again: Rejoice!" (NIV)

51. What book comes before the book of Isaiah?
    A: Song of Solomon (KJV); Song of Songs (NIV)
52. What Bible character said, "What must I do to be saved?"
    A: The jailer—Acts 16:27,29,30
53. How many chapters are there in the book of Jude?
    A: One
54. Who asked Jesus, "Are you the king of the Jews?" (NIV).
    A: Pilate—John 18:33
55. "Trust in the Lord with all thine _____; and lean not unto thine own _____."
    A: Heart, understanding—Proverbs 3:5
56. When the Philistines finally captured Samson, what did they do to him?
    A: Gouged out his eyes—Judges 16:20,21
57. What was the first thing that Adam and Eve did after they sinned?
    A: Sewed fig leaves together "to cover themselves"—Genesis 3:6,7
58. "For nothing is _____ with God" (NIV).
    A: Impossible—Luke 1:37
59. What are the names of the two Bible characters who did not die?
    A: Enoch and Elijah—Genesis 5:24; 2 Kings 2:11
60. "For by grace are ye _____ through _____; and that not of yourselves: it is the gift of God."
    A: Saved, faith—Ephesians 2:8
61. Peter suggests that the day of the Lord will come as a _____.
    A: Thief—2 Peter 3:10
62. What Bible character said, "I am a man of unclean lips"?
    A: Isaiah—Isaiah 6:5
63. What chapter of the Bible is considered the love chapter?
    A: 1 Corinthians 13
64. "The_____says in his heart, 'There is no _____' " (NIV).
    A: Fool, God—Psalm 14:1

65. On the seventh day of creation, what did God do?
    A: Rest—Genesis 2:3
66. Who told the first lie in the Bible?
    A: The serpent—Genesis 3:4,5
67. When Jesus healed the ten lepers, how many returned and thanked Him?
    A: One—Luke 17:15
68. How many days did it take Nehemiah to inspect the city walls of Jerusalem before rebuilding them?
    A: Three—Nehemiah 2:11-13
69. Quote John 1:12.
    A: "But as many as received him, to them gave he power to become the sons of God, even to them that believe on his name."
70. What was the home town of King David?
    A: Bethlehem—1 Samuel 17:12
71. What book comes after the book of Malachi?
    A: Matthew
72. John wrote the book of Revelation on what island?
    A: Patmos—Revelation 1:9-11
73. How many chapters are there in the book of Colossians?
    A: Four
74. In what book of the Bible do we find the words, "Abstain from all appearance of evil"?
    A: 1 Thessalonians—1 Thessalonians 5:22
75. On what mountains did Noah's Ark come to rest?
    A: Ararat—Genesis 8:4
76. What are the names of the two men who wrapped Jesus' body for burial?
    A: Joseph of Arimathea and Nicodemus—John 19:38-40
77. The poor widow in the book of Luke put how many coins into the temple treasury?
    A: Two—Luke 21:2
78. In what book of the Bible do we find the phrase, "The very hairs of your head are all numbered"?
    A: Matthew—Matthew 10:30

79. Who is the author of the book of Zephaniah?
    A: Zephaniah—Zephaniah 1:1
80. Who was the first person to enter the empty tomb of Jesus?
    A: Peter—John 20:4-6
81. Isaiah compares our righteousness to _____ _____.
    A: Filthy rags—Isaiah 64:6
82. What is the number of the beast in the book of Revelation?
    A: Six hundred sixty-six—Revelation 13:18
83. In what book of the Bible do we find the phrase, "Give us this day our daily bread"?
    A: Matthew—Matthew 6:11
84. Who succeeded Moses as leader of the children of Israel?
    A: Joshua—Numbers 27:18-23
85. In what book of the Bible do we find the words, "Without the shedding of blood there is no forgiveness" (NIV)?
    A: Hebrews—Hebrews 9:22
86. Who disguises himself as an angel of light?
    A: Satan—2 Corinthians 11:14
87. When David was a boy, what two fierce animals did he kill?
    A: A lion and a bear—1 Samuel 17:36,37
88. How many years will Satan be bound in the Abyss (bottomless pit)?
    A: One thousand—Revelation 20:2,3
89. What was the name of the type of leaf that Adam and Eve wore before the fall?
    A: They wore nothing before the fall—Genesis 2:25
90. What Bible character originally said, "It is more blessed to give than to receive" (NIV)?
    A: Jesus—Acts 20:35
91. Name the first five people mentioned in the Bible.
    A: Adam, Eve, Cain, Abel, Enoch—Genesis 2:19,20; 3:20; 4:1,2,17
92. How many of the sacrifice sheep did Moses take into the Ark with him?
    A: Moses was not on the Ark.

93. Lydia is known for selling what?
    A: Purple cloth—Acts 16:14
94. What does the Bible say has never been tamed by man?
    A: The human tongue—James 3:8
95. The Bible says there is one thing that never fails. What is it?
    A: Love—1 Corinthians 13:8 (NIV)
96. In what book of the Bible do we find the words, "For my yoke is easy and my burden is light"?
    A: Matthew—Matthew 11:30
97. How many times is the word Bible used in the Bible?
    A: None
98. What book comes after the book of Micah?
    A: Nahum
99. "For where your _____ is, there your _____ will be also" (NIV).
    A: Treasure, heart—Luke 12:34
100. What book comes after the book of Hebrews?
     A: James
101. On what two parts of the body will the mark of the beast be placed?
     A: Forehead or right hand—Revelation 13:16
102. In what book of the Bible do you find the words born again?
     A: John—John 3:3
103. In what book of the Bible is the verse, "Cleanliness is next to godliness"?
     A: It is not in the Bible.
104. Jonah purchased his boat ticket in what city?
     A: Joppa—Jonah 1:3
105. "I can do all things through _____ which _____ me."
     A: Christ, strengtheneth—Philippians 4:13
106. What are the names of the three disciples who were the shortest distance from Jesus in Gethsemane while He prayed?
     A: Peter, James, John—Matthew 26:37

107. In what book of the Bible do we find the words, "If any of you lack wisdom, let him ask of God"?
A: James—James 1:5

108. What is the name of the disciple who was instructed to touch the nail prints in Jesus' hands after His resurrection?
A: Thomas—John 20:25-27

109. What was the name of the angel who spoke to Mary the mother of Jesus?
A: Gabriel—Luke 1:26,27

110. Judas agreed to betray Jesus for how many pieces of silver?
A: Thirty—Matthew 26:14,15

111. What Bible character said, "How can a man be born when he is old?"
A: Nicodemus—John 3:4

112. Who does the Bible say holds the keys of hell and death?
A: Jesus—Revelation 1:18

113. What were the names of the two sisters of Lazarus?
A: Mary and Martha—John 11:1,2

114. What kind of valley is described in Psalm 23?
A: The valley of the shadow of death—Psalm 23:4

115. What Bible character put out a fleece to test God?
A: Gideon—Judges 6:36,37

■ Answers to Fairly Easy Trivia Questions

1. Who was the first Bible character to use a riddle?
   A: Samson—Judges 14:12
2. What was the New Testament word for teacher?
   A: Rabbi or Master—John 1:38
3. What is the name of the man who carried Jesus' cross?
   A: Simon of Cyrene—Matthew 27:32
4. In order for a man to become a bond slave, what did he have to do?
   A: Have his ear pierced—Exodus 21:5,6
5. In speaking of Jesus, who said, "Certainly this was a righteous man"?
   A: The centurion—Luke 23:46,47
6. How many men did Nebuchadnezzar see walking in the fiery furnace?
   A: Four—Daniel 3:24,25
7. In what book of the Bible do we read the words, "Whoso findeth a wife findeth a good thing"?
   A: Proverbs—Proverbs 18:22
8. What was the name of the Bible character who put a veil over his face to hide the glory of God?
   A: Moses—2 Corinthians 3:7,13

9. Jesus was a descendant of what tribe of Israel?
   A: Judah—Hebrews 7:14

10. Saul had a troubled spirit that could only be soothed
    by _____.
    A: Music—1 Samuel 16:15,16

11. The disciples were first called Christians in what city?
    A: Antioch—Acts 11:26

12. What book comes before the book of Joel?
    A: Hosea

13. Who prayed the shortest prayer recorded in the Bible?
    A: Peter—Matthew 14:29,30

14. Quote the shortest prayer in the Bible.
    A: "Lord, save me!"—Matthew 14:30

15. What Bible character said, "What a wretched man I
    am" (NIV)?
    A: Paul the apostle—Romans 7:24

16. What man in the Bible was called the Son of Encourage-
    ment (or consolation)?
    A: Barnabas—Acts 4:36

17. Quote Isaiah 53:6.
    A: "All we like sheep have gone astray; we have turned
    every one to his own way; and the Lord hath laid on him
    the iniquity of us all."

18. In what book of the Bible do we read the words, "Your
    attitude should be the same as that of Christ Jesus" (NIV)?
    A: Philippians—Philippians 2:5

19. "Believe on the Lord Jesus Christ, and thou shalt be
    _____, and thy _____."
    A: Saved, house—Acts 16:31

20. In what book of the Bible do we read the words, "What-
    soever a man soweth, that shall he also reap"?
    A: Galatians—Galatians 6:7

21. What does Proverbs 22 suggest is more desirable than
    great riches?
    A: A good name—Proverbs 22:1

22. What is the name of the first Bible character mentioned drinking wine?
    A: Noah—Genesis 9:20,21
23. What is the number of the largest group of people to whom Christ appeared after His resurrection?
    A: More than 500—1 Corinthians 15:6
24. Name the three Bible characters who are mentioned as fasting for 40 days.
    A: Moses, Elijah, Jesus—Exodus 34:27,28; 1 Kings 19:2,8; Matthew 4:1,2
25. List the books of the Bible that are named after women.
    A: Esther and Ruth
26. Quote Philippians 1:21.
    A: "For to me to live is Christ and to die is gain."
27. If a man hates his son, he will not bother to do what?
    A: Spank him—Proverbs 13:24
28. Which book comes before the book of Obadiah?
    A: Amos
29. What Bible character said, "Here am I; send me"?
    A: Isaiah—Isaiah 6:8
30. The country of Lebanon is famous for what kind of trees?
    A: Cedar—Psalm 104:16
31. _____ was called God's friend.
    A: Abraham—James 2:23
32. According to Timothy, what will people love in the last days?
    A: Themselves, money, and pleasure (NIV); their own selves, pleasures (KJV)—2 Timothy 3:1-5
33. At the time of Christ's birth, who issued a decree for a census (NIV) or tax (KJV)?
    A: Caesar Augustus—Luke 2:1
34. In what book of the Bible do we find the words, "Every man did that which was right in his own eyes"?
    A: Judges—Judges 17:6
35. What book comes after the book of Habakkuk?
    A: Zephaniah

36. How many days after Jesus' resurrection did He ascend to heaven?
    A: Forty—Acts 1:3,9

37. What Bible character called her husband master (lord)?
    A: Sarah—1 Peter 3:6

38. Name the Bible character who was buried by God.
    A: Moses—Deuteronomy 34:5,6

39. According to 2 Timothy, Scripture is profitable for four things. What are they?
    A: Doctrine, reproof, correction, and instruction in righteousness (KJV); teaching, rebuking, correcting, and training in righteousness (NIV)—2 Timothy 3:16

40. What was the name of the father of James and John?
    A: Zebedee—Matthew 4:21

41. Did Hezekiah author the book of Hezekiah?
    A: There is no book of Hezekiah.

42. Jesus told His disciples in the book of Acts that they would be witnesses in three specific locations. What were these locations?
    A: Jerusalem, Judea, Samaria—Acts 1:8

43. What did the rich man in hell want?
    A: Water—Luke 16:22-24

44. Quote 1 Thessalonians 5:16.
    A: "Rejoice evermore."

45. How did God punish Eve for sinning in the Garden of Eden?
    A: Greatly increased pain in childbirth (NIV)—Genesis 3:16

46. In the book of Romans, God is quoted as hating what Bible character?
    A: Esau—Romans 9:13

47. Ananias was told to go to a street called _____.
    A: Straight—Acts 9:11

48. When Joshua entered the Promised Land, what was the name of the second city he attacked?
    A: Ai—Joshua 7:2-5

49. Who was the first man to suggest that Jonah be thrown overboard as a result of the storm?

    A: Jonah—Jonah 1:12

50. What was the name of the Bible character who because of his age slept with a beautiful young virgin in order to keep warm?

    A: King David—1 Kings 1:1-4

51. Which church in the book of Revelation was called lukewarm?

    A: The church at Laodicea—Revelation 3:14-16

52. When the Israelites complained about eating only manna, what did God do?

    A: He sent quail to them—Numbers 11:31

53. Who was the prophet Samuel speaking to when he said, "To obey is better than sacrifice"?

    A: Saul—1 Samuel 15:20,22

54. In the book of Acts, how many men were chosen to wait on tables?

    A: Seven—Acts 6:2,3

55. What is the name of the man who wanted to buy the ability to do miracles like Peter and John?

    A: Simon—Acts 8:18,19

56. Who were the first twins mentioned in the Bible?

    A: Jacob and Esau—Genesis 25:24-26

57. Quote Philippians 4:13.

    A: "I can do all things through Christ which strengtheneth me."

58. What was the name of Adam's son who replaced Abel?

    A: Seth—Genesis 4:25

59. How did the prophet Elijah travel to heaven?

    A: In a whirlwind—2 Kings 2:11

60. Which two New Testament books instruct husbands to love their wives?

    A: Ephesians and Colossians—Ephesians 5:25; Colossians 3:19

61. After Dinah was raped by Shechem, what did her brothers do?
    A: Killed all the men of the city—Genesis 34:25
62. In what book of the Bible do we find the words, "Though your sins are like scarlet, they shall be as white as snow" (NIV)?
    A: Isaiah—Isaiah 1:18
63. King Herod was eaten by _____.
    A: Worms—Acts 12:23
64. In the Old Testament, murderers could flee to what cities in order to be safe?
    A: The cities of refuge—Numbers 35:6
65. Which disciple objected to Mary washing Jesus' feet with perfume?
    A: Judas—John 12:3-5
66. What is the eighth book of the Bible?
    A: Ruth
67. To whom was Paul speaking when he said, "Let no man despise thy youth"?
    A: Timothy—1 Timothy 4:12
68. What is the name of the Pharisee who defended the apostles before the Sanhedrin in the book of Acts?
    A: Gamaliel—Acts 5:34-39
69. Who were the first Gentiles in Caesarea to be converted to Christianity?
    A: Cornelius and his family—Acts 10:30-48
70. What is the name of the queen for whom the Ethiopian eunuch worked?
    A: Candace—Acts 8:27
71. Which is the longest book in the New Testament?
    a. Matthew   b. Luke   c. Romans   d. Revelation
    A: "B" or Luke
72. What is the name of the Bible character who said, "Let me inherit a double portion of your spirit" (NIV)?
    A: Elisha—2 Kings 2:9

73. When Philip met the Ethiopian eunuch, he was reading from the book of which prophet?
    A: Isaiah (NIV); Esaias (KJV)—Acts 8:26-28
74. Quote 1 Thessalonians 5:18.
    A: "In every thing give thanks: for this is the will of God in Christ Jesus concerning you."
75. In the book of Philemon, what is the name of the servant for whom Paul was making an appeal?
    A: Onesimus—Philemon 10
76. What were the names of Job's three friends?
    A: Eliphaz, Bildad, Zophar—Job 2:11
77. As a result of Adam's sin, what became cursed?
    A: The ground—Genesis 3:17
78. Who does James suggest will be judged more strictly than others?
    A: Teachers (NIV); masters (KJV)—James 3:1
79. What is the name of the man whom King David made drunk?
    A: Uriah—2 Samuel 11:12,13
80. The book of Romans has how many chapters?
    A: Sixteen
81. Lydia, the seller of purple, was from which city?
    A: Thyatira—Acts 16:14
82. In what book of the Bible did Paul state that people who do not work should not eat?
    A: 2 Thessalonians—2 Thessalonians 3:10
83. What New Testament book tells the story of a man eating a book (or scroll)?
    A: Revelation—Revelation 10:9,10
84. In what book of the Bible does it talk about Satan accusing believers before God day and night?
    A: Revelation—Revelation 12:10
85. In the book of Acts, what was the name of the man who predicted that a famine would spread over the entire Roman world?
    A: Agabus—Acts 11:28

86. What does Proverbs say is a mocker?
    A: Wine—Proverbs 20:1
87. The word Armageddon is used only one time in Scripture. In what book of the Bible is this word found?
    A: Revelation—Revelation 16:16
88. In what book in the Bible does it suggest that we not eat too much honey?
    A: Proverbs—Proverbs 25:16
89. In the book of Colossians there was a man named Justus. What was his famous other name?
    A: Jesus—Colossians 4:11
90. Who was the first person mentioned in the Bible as laughing?
    A: Sarah—Genesis 18:12,13
91. What does the Bible say was put in charge to bring us to Christ before faith came?
    A: The law—Galatians 3:23,24
92. When David had to face Goliath, he picked up:
    a. Three rough stones   b. Five smooth stones
    c. Five rough stones   d. Three smooth stones
    A: "B" or five smooth stones—1 Samuel 17:40
93. Which one of Noah's sons looked on Noah's nakedness?
    A: Ham—Genesis 9:22
94. What is the name of the priest that Abram met in the valley of Shaveh?
    A: Melchizedek—Genesis 14:17,18
95. What is the name of the land that God told Abram to leave?
    A: Ur of the Chaldeans—Genesis 15:7
96. In 1 Corinthians, what is the last enemy to be destroyed?
    A: Death—1 Corinthians 15:26
97. Which of these did Jesus cure first?
    a. Blindness   b. Leprosy   c. Lameness
    A: "B" or leprosy—Matthew 8:2,3
98. What was the name of the man who made a metal snake and put it on a pole?
    A: Moses—Numbers 21:9

99. In what book of the Bible do you find the words, "Remember your Creator in the days of your youth" (NIV)?
A: Ecclesiastes—Ecclesiastes 12:1

100. Quote Romans 8:28.
A: "And we know that all things work together for good to them that love God, to them who are called according to his purpose."

101. The book of Proverbs suggests that a good medicine is a _____ _____.
A: Cheerful heart (NIV); merry heart (KJV)—Proverbs 17:22

102. When blind Bartimaeus came to Jesus, he threw something away. What was it?
A: His cloak—Mark 10:49,50

103. An Israelite man was exempt from war for how long after he was married?
A: One year—Deuteronomy 24:5

104. King Herod killed all the baby boys in Bethlehem who were _____ years old and under.
A: Two—Matthew 2:16

105. What was the name of an angel that fought with the dragon in the book of Revelation?
A: Michael—Revelation 12:7

106. What was the name of Solomon's mother?
A: Bathsheba—2 Samuel 12:24

107. What did the angels do to the homosexual men of Sodom to protect Lot?
A: They struck them with blindness—Genesis 19:9-11

108. Why did Adam name his wife Eve?
A: Because she was mother of all the living—Genesis 3:20

109. Who said, "I am slow of speech, and of a slow tongue"?
A: Moses—Exodus 4:10

110. What two things did God say would happen to Eve for disobedience in the Garden of Eden?
A: Greatly increased pain in childbearing, her husband would rule over her (NIV); multiplied sorrow in childbirth, her husband would rule over her (KJV)—Genesis 3:16

111. Who said there is "a time to weep and a time to laugh"?
     A: Solomon—Ecclesiastes 3:4
112. In the book of Revelation, who held the key to the Abyss (bottomless pit)?
     A: An angel—Revelation 20:1
113. Who said, "How beautiful are the feet of them that preach the gospel of peace"?
     A: Isaiah—Isaiah 52:7; Paul—Romans 10:15
114. Who wore golden bells on the hem of a blue robe?
     A: Aaron—Exodus 28:31-35
115. What was the name of the Bible character who had red hair like a garment all over his body?
     A: Esau—Genesis 25:25
116. When Apollos came from Alexandria, he first preached in what city?
     A: Ephesus—Acts 18:24-26
117. In what New Testament book do you find the words, "What therefore God hath joined together let not man put asunder"?
     A: Mark—Mark 10:9
118. Philip had four daughters who had a special spiritual gift. What was that gift?
     A: Prophecy—Acts 21:8,9
119. What is the name of the only man mentioned in the Bible as being bald-headed?
     A: Elisha—2 Kings 2:22,23
120. When the angel in the book of Revelation came to bind Satan, what two objects did he have in his hand?
     A: Key and chain—Revelation 20:1,2
121. Jesus calls Himself the morning star in what book of the Bible?
     A: Revelation—Revelation 22:16
122. What Bible character describes his girlfriend's hair as a flock of goats descending from Gilead?
     A: Solomon—Song of Solomon 6:5
123. After Jesus' trial, what color of robe was put on Him?
     A: Purple—Mark 15:15-17

124. Which book of the Bible says, "I would rather be a doorkeeper in the house of my God than dwell in the tents of the wicked" (NIV)?

A: Psalms—Psalm 84:10

125. What is the thirtieth book of the Bible?

A: Amos

126. Quote Philippians 4:19.

A: "But my God shall supply all your needs according to his riches in glory by Christ Jesus."

■ Answers to Fairly Difficult Trivia Questions

1. What is the name of the Bible character who went to visit the witch of Endor?
   A: King Saul—1 Samuel 28:7,8
2. A Christian who returns to a life of sin is likened to which animals?
   A: A dog and a sow—2 Peter 2:20-22
3. In what book of the Bible does it talk about blood running so deep that it reaches up to the bridles of horses?
   A: Revelation—Revelation 14:20
4. The furnace into which Shadrach, Meshach, and Abednego were tossed was heated how many times hotter than usual?
   A: Seven—Daniel 3:19
5. How many times did Jacob bow as he approached Esau?
   A: Seven—Genesis 33:1-3
6. What were the names of the two believers who discipled Apollos?
   A: Priscilla and Aquila—Acts 18:24-26
7. What was the name of Mordecai's cousin whom he brought up?
   A: Esther or Hadassah—Esther 2:7

8. What is the name of the tree that stands on both sides
of the river of the water of life in the book of Revelation?
A: The tree of life—Revelation 22:1,2

9. What is the name of the Bible character who got leprosy
by sticking his hand inside his cloak?
A: Moses—Exodus 4:6

10. Jesus said He could call on His Father for how many
legions of angels?
A: More than 12—Matthew 26:53

11. What was the occupation of Jairus?
A: He was a ruler of the synagogue—Luke 8:41

12. In what two books of the Bible do we find the phrase,
"Be not weary in well doing"?
A: 2 Thessalonians and Galatians—2 Thessalonians 3:13;
Galatians 6:9

13. What was the first command the Bible mentions that God
gave to Adam and Eve?
A: Be fruitful and multiply—Genesis 1:28

14. What was the name of the Bible character who was called
"mighty in the Scriptures"?
A: Apollos—Acts 18:24

15. The Year of Jubilee comes how often for the Israelites?
A: Every 50 years—Leviticus 25:10,11

16. What will the gates of the holy city be made of?
A: Pearls—Revelation 21:21

17. How many bowls of water did Gideon squeeze out of his
fleece?
A: One—Judges 6:38

18. Satan smote Job with_____from the soles
of his feet to the top of his head.
A: Painful sores (NIV); sore boils (KJV)—Job 2:7

19. Who suggested that it is not wise to spend too much time
at your neighbor's house?
A: Solomon—Proverbs 25:17

20. What Bible character said, "Almost thou persuadest me to
be a Christian"?
A: King Agrippa—Acts 26:27,28

21. David took two things from Saul while he was asleep. What were they?
    A: A spear and a waterjug—1 Samuel 26:7,12

22. What is the name of the Bible character who took all of the gold articles out of Solomon's temple?
    A: Nebuchadnezzar—2 Kings 24:11,13

23. In what book of the Bible do we read the words, "It is required in stewards that a man be found faithful"?
    A: 1 Corinthians—1 Corinthians 4:2

24. Where did Job live?
    a. Puz   b. Buz   c. Uz   d. Luz   e. Zuz
    A: "C" or Uz—Job 1:1

25. What was the name of Elisha's servant?
    A: Gehazi—2 Kings 4:25

26. In what book of the Bible do we find the story about the sun standing still?
    A: Joshua—Joshua 10:12-14

27. Which men wanted to kill Lazarus?
    A: The chief priests—John 12:10

28. What color was manna?   a. Yellowish   b. Reddish
    c. Brownish   d. White
    A: "D" or white—Exodus 16:31

29. What two items that touched Paul were then used to heal people?
    A: Handkerchiefs and aprons—Acts 19:11,12

30. In the Promised Land there were _____ cities of refuge.
    A: Six—Numbers 35:6

31. Where does the Bible suggest that too much study is hard on the body?
    A: Ecclesiastes—Ecclesiastes 12:12

32. Ruth and Boaz had a son named _____.
    A: Obed—Ruth 4:13-17

33. In what book of the Bible do we find the words, "He who wins souls is wise" (NIV)?
    A: Proverbs—Proverbs 11:30

34. Zacchaeus repaid to the people he had cheated how many times the amount?
    A: Four—Luke 19:8

35. Name the New Testament book that was written to Gaius.
    A: 3 John

36. In what book of the Bible do we read the words, "For the love of money is the root of all evil"?
    A: 1 Timothy—1 Timothy 6:10

37. The poles used in carrying the Ark of the Covenant were made out of what kind of wood?
    A: Acacia (NIV); shittim (KJV)—Exodus 25:10-16

38. What was the other name of the Bible character called Didymus?
    A: Thomas—John 20:24

39. Who is the judge and defender of widows?
    A: God—Psalm 68:5

40. Does the Bible say that husbands should submit to their wives?
    A: Yes—Ephesians 5:21

41. Who said that the Jews had holes in their purses?
    A: God, through the prophet Haggai—Haggai 1:6

42. Who is likened to a gold ring in a pig's snout?
    A: A beautiful woman lacking discretion—Proverbs 11:22

43. At what time of day did Eutychus go to sleep and fall out of the window?
    A: Midnight—Acts 20:7-9

44. In what book of the Bible do you find the words, "It is more blessed to give than to receive"?
    A: Acts—Acts 20:35

45. What two men were candidates for the position of the twelfth apostle after Judas' death?
    A: Joseph (called Barsabbas) and Matthias—Acts 1:23

46. What is the name of the man who replaced Judas as the twelfth apostle?
    A: Matthias—Acts 1:26

47. Earthly treasures are destroyed by three things. What are they?
    A: Moths, rust, and thieves—Matthew 6:19
48. In what book of the Bible do you find the words, "Man looks at the outward appearance, but the Lord looks at the heart" (NIV)?
    A: 1 Samuel—1 Samuel 16:7
49. According to Proverbs, the tongue of the wise brings what?
    A: Healing (NIV); health (KJV)—Proverbs 12:18
50. At what time of day is it not good to loudly bless your neighbor?
    A: Early in the morning—Proverbs 27:14
51. How many horns did the goat in Daniel's second vision have?
    A: One—Daniel 8:5
52. What was the name of Moses' father?
    A: Amram—Exodus 6:20
53. Who said, "But godliness with contentment is great gain"?
    A: Paul—1 Timothy 6:6
54. In what book of the Bible are we told to cast our bread upon the waters?
    A: Ecclesiastes—Ecclesiastes 11:1
55. What was the name of the boy who was left under a bush to die?
    A: Ishmael—Genesis 16:16; 21:14-16
56. In order to be on the church widow's list, how old did a widow need to be?
    A: Sixty years old—1 Timothy 5:9
57. What was on each of the four corners of the bronze altar in the tabernacle?
    A: A horn—Exodus 27:2
58. The book of 1 Chronicles spends most of its pages discussing which Bible character?
    A: David
59. King Og's bed was made of what kind of metal?
    a. Gold   b. Iron   c. Silver   d. Steel   e. Brass

A: "B" or Iron—Deuteronomy 3:11

60. Paul asked Timothy to bring him two items while he was in prison. What were those items?
    A: Cloak and scrolls (books—KJV)—2 Timothy 4:13

61. What woman in the Bible faked a rape because she was mad?
    A: Potiphar's wife—Genesis 39:10-15

62. What was Tabitha's other name?
    A: Dorcas—Acts 9:36

63. What did Jesus and His disciples cross just before He was arrested?
    A: The Kidron Valley (NIV); the brook Cedron (KJV)— John 18:1-3

64. What does the Bible say cannot be bought for any price?
    A: Love—Song of Solomon 8:7

65. The Bible says that male babies should be circumcised when they are how old?
    A: Eight days—Leviticus 12:3

66. What is the name of the servant girl who answered the door when Peter escaped from prison?
    A: Rhoda—Acts 12:13

67. In the story of the rich man and Lazarus, how many brothers did the rich man have?
    A: Five—Luke 16:27,28

68. How old was Isaac when he married Rebekah?
    A: Forty—Genesis 25:20

69. When the kings of the East march westward, what river will dry up?
    A: Euphrates—Revelation 16:12

70. What does "manna" mean?
    A: "What is it?"—Exodus 16:15

71. What are the names of the two women who fought over who would eat mandrakes?
    A: Leah and Rachel—Genesis 30:14-16

72. Where was the only place a Nazarite could cut his hair?
    A: At the entrance to the Tent of Meeting (NIV); at the door of the tabernacle (KJV)—Numbers 6:18

73. The book of Proverbs names four things that are stately in their stride. What are they?
    A: A lion, a rooster (greyhound—KJV), a he-goat, a king—Proverbs 30:29-31

74. In the book of Acts, Peter had a vision that repeated itself how many times?
    A: Three—Acts 10:9-16

75. In the book of Revelation, what spice did the merchants of the earth sell to Babylon?
    A: Cinnamon—Revelation 18:11-13

76. Paul the apostle was stoned in what city?
    A: Lystra—Acts 14:8-19

77. What is the name of the man who was ready to kill his son because he ate honey?
    A: Saul—1 Samuel 14:43,44

78. What is the name of the man who was to provide for the needs of Mephibosheth?
    A: Ziba—2 Samuel 9:9,10

79. Manoah had a famous son. What was his name?
    A: Samson—Judges 13:2,3,24

80. When Abimelech set fire to the tower of Shechem, how many people died in the flames?
    A: About 1000—Judges 9:47-49

81. Who does the Bible say goes around and whispers, peeps, and mutters?
    A: Mediums and spiritists (NIV); wizards (KJV)—Isaiah 8:19,20

82. In what book of the Bible do we find mention of a mother eagle stirring up her nest?
    A: Deuteronomy—Deuteronomy 32:11

83. Who was the first person mentioned in the Bible as being put into prison?
    A: Joseph—Genesis 39:20

84. In which book of the Bible do we find mention of a synagogue of Satan?
    A: Revelation—Revelation 2:9

85. In the Old Testament, what particular people could not "make baldness upon their head" or cut off the edges of their beards?
    A: Priests—Leviticus 21:5
86. Who said that we should not curse rich people from our bedroom?
    A: Solomon—Ecclesiastes 10:20
87. How many times is the phrase "born again" mentioned in the Bible?
    A: Two—John 3:3,7
88. How many times does the word trinity appear in the Bible?
    A: None
89. What Bible character fell on his face and laughed?
    A: Abraham—Genesis 17:17
90. What Bible character said that laughter is mad (or foolish—NIV)?
    A: Solomon—Ecclesiastes 2:2
91. Who said that even in laughter the heart is sorrowful (aches)?
    A: Solomon—Proverbs 14:13
92. In what book of the Bible does it say that, "A feast is made for laughter"?
    A: Ecclesiastes—Ecclesiastes 10:19
93. What Bible character said, "Let your laughter be turned to mourning"?
    A: James—James 4:9
94. What Bible character said, "The fear of the Lord, that is wisdom; and to depart from evil is understanding"?
    A: Job—Job 28:28
95. What caused the flood waters to recede from the face of the earth?
    A: A wind—Genesis 8:1
96. How many years did Noah live after the flood?
    A: Three hundred fifty—Genesis 9:28
97. What kind of grain did Boaz give to Ruth?
    A: Barley—Ruth 3:15

98. In the book of Exodus, what was the color of the priest's robe?
    A: Blue—Exodus 28:31
99. Saul was hiding in the _____ when he was to be presented as the king of Israel.
    A: Baggage (NIV)—1 Samuel 10:21-24
100. What was the name of Aaron's wife?
    A: Elisheba—Exodus 6:23
101. Jesus was a high priest after the order of _____.
    A: Melchizedek—Hebrews 5:5,6
102. Paul and Silas prayed at what time of day while they were in jail?
    A: Midnight—Acts 16:25
103. In what book of the Bible do you find the statement, "Thy navel is like a round goblet"?
    A: Song of Solomon (Song of Songs—NIV)—Song of Solomon 7:2
104. Who were called, "Liars, evil beasts, slow bellies"?
    A: The Cretans—Titus 1:12
105. In the book of Luke, who took away the key of knowledge?
    A: The lawyers—Luke 11:52
106. In what book of the Bible do we find the first mention of a holy kiss?
    A: Romans—Romans 16:16
107. Who sneezed seven times in the Bible?
    A: The Shunammite's son—2 Kings 4:35,36
108. In which book of the Bible do we find the country of Spain mentioned?
    A: Romans—Romans 15:24,28
109. In what book of the Bible do we find mention of birthing stools?
    A: Exodus—Exodus 1:15-17
110. God said that anyone who would kill Cain would receive from Him _____ vengeance.
    a. Threefold   b. Sevenfold   c. Tenfold
    A: "B" or sevenfold—Genesis 4:15
111. What were the names of Noah's three daughters-in-law?

A: The Bible does not say.

112. What was the sign of the covenant between Abram and God?
A: Circumcision—Genesis 17:9-14

113. Who said, "Is anything too hard for the Lord?" (NIV)
A: God Himself—Genesis 18:13,14

114. What did Lot offer to the men of the city of Sodom so they would not take the two angels?
A: His two daughters—Genesis 19:6-8

115. The division of angels called seraphs (seraphims—KJV) have how many wings?
A: Six—Isaiah 6:2

116. Who was called the king of righteousness in the book of Hebrews?
A: Melchizedek—Hebrews 7:1,2

117. In what book of the Bible does it talk about God giving names to all of the stars?
A: Psalms—Psalm 147:4

118. Name the city in which Paul had his hair cut off because of a vow.
A: Cenchrea—Acts 18:18

119. On the sixth day the children of Israel were to gather how many omers of manna for each person?
A: Two—Exodus 16:22

120. Who had the first navy mentioned in the Bible?
A: King Solomon—1 Kings 9:26,27

121. To whom did Jesus say, "Thou gavest me no kiss"?
A: Simon the Pharisee—Luke 7:44,45

122. In the book of Proverbs, the virtuous woman clothed her entire family in what color?
A: Scarlet—Proverbs 31:21

123. What was the former name for the town of Bethel?
A: Luz—Judges 1:23

124. The eighth plague that the Egyptians experienced was the plague of locusts. A strong wind carried the locusts away in which direction?
A: East into the Red Sea—Exodus 10:19

■ Answers to Hard Trivia Questions

1. Whose birthday celebration was the first mentioned in the Bible?
   A: Pharaoh's—Genesis 40:20
2. In what book of the Bible does it talk about trading a boy for a harlot?
   A: Joel—Joel 3:3
3. How many men in the Bible were named Judas?
   A: Six—Matthew 10:4; 13:55; Luke 6:16; Acts 5:37; 9:11; 15:22
4. Who received the first kiss that is mentioned in the Bible?
   A: Isaac—Genesis 27:26,27
5. "The men of _____ were wicked and sinners before the Lord exceedingly."
   A: Sodom—Genesis 13:13
6. In what book of the Bible do we find the first mention of a physician?
   A: Jeremiah—Jeremiah 8:22
7. When Jeremiah said that all their heads would be shaved and their beards clipped, who was he speaking about?
   A: Moab—Jeremiah 48:36,37

8. Whose lips quivered and bones decayed when he heard the voice of the Lord?
   A: Habakkuk—Habakkuk 3:16

9. In what book of the Bible do you find the words, "Thine eyes like the fishpools in Heshbon"?
   A: Song of Solomon (Song of Songs-NIV)—Song of Solomon 7:4

10. Who was the first man mentioned in the Bible as dreaming?
    A: Abimelech—Genesis 20:3

11. In what book of the Bible do we find God's punishment of "consumption, and the burning ague"?
    A: Leviticus—Leviticus 26:16

12. How many chapters are in the book of Esther?
    A: Ten

13. How much money did the innkeeper receive from the Good Samaritan for taking care of the sick man?
    A: Two silver coins (NIV); two pence—about 15 cents (KJV)—Luke 10:35

14. In what book of the Bible do we find the first mention of a "lunatic"?
    A: Matthew—Matthew 4:24

15. King Solomon had how many horsemen?
    A: Twelve thousand—2 Chronicles 9:25

16. In what book of the Bible do we have the first mention of magicians?
    A: Genesis—Genesis 41:8

17. Who does the Bible say eats, wipes her mouth, and says, "I've done nothing wrong"?
    A: An adulteress—Proverbs 30:20

18. What did David do with Goliath's weapons?
    A: He kept them—1 Samuel 17:54

19. In the end of the book of Job, how many camels did God give to Job?
    A: Six thousand—Job 42:12

20. When Elijah built the altar on Mount Carmel, how many stones did he use?
    A: Twelve—1 Kings 18:31,32

21. What were the names of Pharaoh's two store cities in the book of Exodus?
   A: Pithom, Rameses—Exodus 1:11
22. In the book of Ruth, what was Naomi's other name?
   A: Mara—Ruth 1:20
23. In what book of the Bible does God say there will be showers of blessing?
   A: Ezekiel—Ezekiel 34:26
24. In which book of the Bible do you read the words, "Be sure your sin will find you out"?
   A: Numbers—Numbers 32:23
25. Nabal owned how many goats?
   A: One thousand—1 Samuel 25:2,3
26. When Josiah heard God's law read, he did what?
   A: Tore his robes—2 Chronicles 34:19
27. In what book of the Bible do we find mention of 20,000 baths of wine and 20,000 baths of oil?
   A: 2 Chronicles—2 Chronicles 2:10
28. In Zechariah's vision of four chariots, what was the color of the horses pulling the fourth chariot?
   A: Dappled (NIV); grisled and bay (KJV)—Zechariah 6:1-3
29. One book in the Bible has the same amount of chapters as there are books in the Bible. What is the name of the book?
   A: Isaiah
30. What was the name of Jonah's father?
   A: Amittai—Jonah 1:1
31. How many chapters are in the book of Nehemiah?
   A: Thirteen
32. What was the occupation of Shiphrah and Puah?
   A: They were Hebrew midwives—Exodus 1:15
33. What animal was never to be cooked in its mother's milk?
   A: A young goat—Exodus 23:19
34. Rahab the harlot hid the two Jewish spies under what?
   A: Flax—Joshua 2:1-6

35. What are the names of the two women who argued over who would get to sleep with their mutual husband?
    A: Leah and Rachel—Genesis 30:14-16
36. Miriam played what kind of musical instrument?
    A: Tambourine (NIV); timbrel (KJV)—Exodus 15:20
37. What does the Bible say manna tasted like?
    A: Wafers with honey—Exodus 16:31; olive oil (NIV)—Numbers 11:8
38. What Bible character was called a wild donkey of a man?
    A: Hagar's son Ishmael (NIV)—Genesis 16:7-12
39. When King Nebuchadnezzar went crazy, his fingernails began to look like _____.
    A: Birds' claws—Daniel 4:33,34
40. What is the last word in the Bible?
    A: Amen—Revelation 22:21
41. What Bible character fell in love with his sister?
    A: Amnon—2 Samuel 13:1,2
42. The prophet Amos tended two things. What were they?
    A: Sheep and sycamore trees—Amos 7:14
43. The Ark of the Testimony or Covenant was covered with what color cloth when it was moved?
    A: Blue—Numbers 4:5,6
44. Who was the first Bible character mentioned as living in a tent?
    A: Jabal—Genesis 4:20
45. What is the name of the Bible character who ran faster than a chariot?
    A: Elijah—1 Kings 18:45,46
46. What three colors were used in sewing the tabernacle curtains?
    A: Blue, purple, and scarlet—Exodus 26:1
47. Who came out with bald heads and raw shoulders after a long siege against the city of Tyre?
    A: Nebuchadnezzar's soldiers—Ezekiel 29:18
48. At what time of day did the sailors going to Rome on the ship with Paul first sense land after the storm?
    A: Midnight—Acts 27:20-27

49. In the book of Acts, how many soldiers guarded Peter while he was in prison?
    A: Sixteen (NIV)—Acts 12:3,4

50. Who was the first man in the Bible mentioned as being sick?
    A: Jacob—Genesis 48:1,2

51. Who was the fourth oldest man in the Bible?
    A: Adam—Genesis 5:5,20,27; 9:29

52. How many yoke of oxen did Job own before tragedy entered his life?
    A: Five hundred—Job 1:3

53. In Elim, the Israelites found 70 palm trees and _____ springs (fountains).
    A: Twelve—Numbers 33:9

54. Moses was told by the Lord to write what on the staff of each leader of the tribes of Israel?
    A: The leader's name—Numbers 17:1,2

55. Hannah was taunted by_____about not having a baby.
    A: Peninnah—1 Samuel 1:2,4-6

56. Certain Athenian philosophers thought Paul the apostle was a _____.
    A: Babbler—Acts 17:18

57. Zechariah had a vision of a basket (ephah). What was in the basket?
    A: A woman—Zechariah 5:7

58. When King Shishak stole the gold shields from the temple, who replaced them with bronze (brass) shields?
    A: Rehoboam—2 Chronicles 12:9,10

59. In what book of the Bible do we find mention of the name Narcissus?
    A: Romans—Romans 16:11

60. In what book of the Bible do you find the words, "The joy of the Lord is your strength"?
    A: Nehemiah—Nehemiah 8:10

61. Who is the first person in the Bible mentioned as writing a letter?
    A: David—2 Samuel 11:14
62. Who received the first letter written in the Bible?
    A: Joab—2 Samuel 11:14
63. Who said, "If I perish, I perish"?
    A: Esther—Esther 4:15,16
64. Name the shortest book in the Old Testament.
    a. Jonah   b. Nehemiah   c. Obadiah
    d. Zephaniah   e. Malachi
    A: "C" or Obadiah—21 verses
65. The Recabites refused to drink_____.
    A: Wine—Jeremiah 35:5,6
66. The woman who poured perfume on Jesus' head carried the perfume in what kind of jar?
    A: An alabaster jar (NIV)—Matthew 26:6,7
67. Who does the Bible say was the most humble man?
    A: Moses—Numbers 12:3
68. Who was Asenath's famous husband?
    A: Joseph—Genesis 41:45
69. Who bored a hole in the lid of a chest so that it could become a bank to hold money?
    A: Jehoiada the priest—2 Kings 12:9
70. After feeding the 4000 men, Jesus went where?
    A: The vicinity of Magadan (NIV); the coasts of Magdala (KJV)—Matthew 15:38,39
71. What is the name of the prophet who said that Paul would be arrested in Jerusalem?
    A: Agabus—Acts 21:10,11
72. When the temple in the Old Testament was moved, what kind of animal skins were put over the Ark of the Testimony or Covenant?
    A: Hides of sea cows (NIV); badgers' skins (KJV)—Numbers 4:5,6
73. What was the name of the dying king who was propped up in his chariot for a whole day?
    A: Ahab—1 Kings 22:34,35,40

74. The Anakites (Anakims-KJV) and the Emites (Emims-KJV) had a common physical characteristic. What was it?
   A: Their tall stature—Deuteronomy 2:10

75. King Solomon had his carriage upholstered in what color of material?
   A: Purple—Song of Solomon 3:9,10

76. In which book of the Bible do we find the first mention of the name Satan?
   A: 1 Chronicles—1 Chronicles 21:1

77. The invalid had been lying by the pool of Bethesda for how many years?
   A: Thirty-eight—John 5:2-5

78. Mary washed Jesus' feet with what kind of perfume?
   A: Nard (NIV); spikenard (KJV)—John 12:3

79. What did Jacob name the place where he wrestled with a man?
   A: Peniel—Genesis 32:24,30

80. When Jacob wrestled with a man, what were the man's first words to Jacob?
   A: "Let me go, for the day breaketh"—Genesis 32:24-26

81. How many men did Esau bring with him when he came to meet Jacob?
   a. 100   b. 200   c. 300   d. 400   e. 500
   A: "D" or four hundred—Genesis 32:6

82. What special physical feature did Leah have?
   A: Her eyes—Genesis 29:17

83. Elisha was plowing the ground with how many yoke of oxen when Elijah found him?
   A: Twelve—1 Kings 19:19

84. In what book of the Bible does it talk about people who could not tell their right hand from their left hand?
   A: Jonah—Jonah 4:11

85. What is the name of the man who raped Dinah?
   A: Shechem—Genesis 34:1,2

86. When Job became ill, his skin turned to what color?
   A: Black—Job 30:30

87. David's delegation to King Hanun had to stay in what town until their beards had grown back?
    A: Jericho—1 Chronicles 19:1-5
88. What woman's name is mentioned most often in the Bible?
    A: Sarah—60 times
89. Gideon was the father of how many sons?
    A: Seventy-one—Judges 8:29-31,35
90. What is the name of the king who had 900 iron chariots?
    A: King Jabin—Judges 4:2,3
91. King Solomon had how many steps to his throne?
    A: Six—1 Kings 10:18-20
92. What was the name of Isaiah's father?
    A: Amoz—Isaiah 1:1
93. David was betrothed to Saul's daughter for how many Philistine foreskins?
    A: One hundred—2 Samuel 3:14
94. After the Philistines cut off Saul's head, they put it in the temple of _____.
    A: Dagon—1 Chronicles 10:8-10
95. Deborah, the Old Testament judge, sat under what kind of tree?
    A: Palm—Judges 4:4,5
96. In the parable of the Good Samaritan, who was the second person to ignore the injured man?
    A: A Levite—Luke 10:30-32
97. When King Ben-Hadad attacked Samaria, how many kings helped him?
    A: Thirty-two—1 Kings 20:1
98. Jonathan, Ishvi, and Malki-Shua had a famous father. What was his name?
    A: Saul—1 Samuel 14:49
99. What is the name of the Bible prophet who was lifted by his hair between heaven and earth to see a vision?
    A: Ezekiel—Ezekiel 8:3
100. What name did Amos call the sinful women of Israel?
    A: Cows of Bashan (NIV)—Amos 4:1

101. Nehemiah went to the keeper of the king's forest to get wood. What was the forest-keeper's name?
A: Asaph—Nehemiah 2:8

102. When is the first time love is mentioned in the Bible?
A: When Isaac married Rebekah—Genesis 24:67

103. In which book of the Bible do we find the only mention of the name Lucifer?
A: Isaiah—Isaiah 14:12

104. What Bible character said, "By my God have I leaped over a wall"?
A: David—Psalm 18:29

105. Who was the first left-handed man mentioned in the Bible?
A: Ehud the left-handed Benjamite—Judges 3:15

106. Who called Israel a "backsliding heifer"?
A: Hosea—Hosea 4:16

107. Who said, "Man is born into trouble, as the sparks fly upward"?
A: Eliphaz the Temanite—Job 4:1; 5:7

108. The river Pishon flowed out of the Garden of Eden into the land of _____, where there was gold.
A: Havilah—Genesis 2:10,11

109. In what book of the Bible do we find mention of the word stargazers?
A: Isaiah—Isaiah 47:13

110. The name "Ziz" was _____.
a. A city   b. A brook   c. A cliff   d. A soldier
e. A priest   f. None of the above
A: "C" or a cliff—2 Chronicles 20:16

111. Jazer was _____.
a. A king   b. A land   c. A priest   d. A river
e. A servant   f. None of the above
A: "B" or a land—Numbers 32:1

112. How old was Adam when he died?
A: Nine hundred and thirty—Genesis 5:5

113. Who was the father of Enoch?
A: Jared—Genesis 5:18

114. How many days after the tops of the mountains appeared

did Noah wait before he opened the window of the Ark?
A: Forty—Genesis 8:5,6

115. Who was the famous son of Terah?
A: Abram—Genesis 11:26

116. When Lot left Sodom, what city did he flee to?
A: Zoar—Genesis 19:18-22

117. What are the names of the two children who were born to Lot's two daughters?
A: Moab and Ben-Ammi—Genesis 19:36-38

118. How old was Sarah when she died?
a. 103   b. 112   c. 127   d. 133
A: "C" or 127—Genesis 23:1

119. What were the names of the two wives of Esau who caused Isaac and Rebekah much grief?
A: Judith and Basemath—Genesis 26:34,35

120. Who was the second oldest man in the Bible?
A: Jared—Genesis 5:20,27

121. How old was Enoch when God took him to heaven?
A: Three hundred and sixty-five—Genesis 5:23,24

122. The Israelites hung their harps on what kind of trees?
A: Poplars (NIV); willows (KJV)—Psalm 137:2

123. After baptizing the eunuch, Philip was taken by the Spirit of the Lord to what city?
A: Azotus—Acts 8:38-40

124. How long did Job live after the Lord made him prosperous again?
A: One hundred and forty years—Job 42:16

125. What was the name of Eli's grandson?
A: Ichabod—1 Samuel 4:16-21

■ Answers to Trivia Questions for the Expert

1. Who were the men of whom God said, "Thou shalt make for them girdles, and bonnets"?
   A: Aaron's sons—Exodus 28:40
2. Which book in the Bible talks about men who "belch out with their mouth"?
   A: Psalms—Psalm 59:7
3. In what book of the Bible does it talk about ice coming out of the womb?
   A: Job—Job 38:29
4. Who laughed when threatened with a spear?
   A: God—Job 41:29
5. In what book of the Bible do we find mention of "wimples and the crisping pins"?
   A: Isaiah—Isaiah 3:22
6. What is the name of the Bible character who had 30 sons who rode on 30 donkeys and controlled 30 cities?
   A: Jair—Judges 10:3,4
7. In what book of the Bible do we have the first mention of a barber's razor?
   A: Numbers—Numbers 6:5

8. The angel of the Lord killed how many of Sennacherib's soldiers?
   A: One hundred eighty-five thousand—Isaiah 37:36,37

9. How many times is the Old Testament quoted in the book of Revelation?
   A: Two hundred and forty-five

10. In what verse of the Bible do we find the word "canker-worm" mentioned twice?
    A: Nahum 3:15

11. In what book of the Bible do we find the only two occurrences of the word rainbow?
    A: Revelation—Revelation 4:3; 10:1

12. In what book of the Bible do we read the words, "Twisting the nose produces blood" (NIV)?
    A: Proverbs—Proverbs 30:33

13. What is the name of the Bible character who said, "I have escaped with only the skin of my teeth" (NIV)?
    A: Job—Job 19:20

14. According to King Solomon, good news gives health to what part of our body?
    A: Bones—Proverbs 15:30

15. How long did Ezekiel lie on his right side for the sins of Judah?
    A: Forty days—Ezekiel 4:6

16. What book of the Bible talks about "five gold tumors and five gold rats" (NIV)?
    A: 1 Samuel—1 Samuel 6:4

17. The bronze snake that Moses made was broken into pieces by what king?
    A: Hezekiah—2 Kings 18:1-4

18. What Bible character was smothered to death by a wet cloth?
    A: Ben-Hadad (NIV)—2 Kings 8:14,15

19. Which chapter in the book of Psalms could be a statement against abortion?
    A: Psalm 139—Psalm 139:13-16

20. What book of the Bible talks about a man "that hath a flat nose"?
    A: Leviticus—Leviticus 21:18
21. What Bible character was known for his threats to gouge out the right eye of the people who lived in Jabesh Gilead?
    A: Nahash—1 Samuel 11:1,2
22. How close to the city of Jericho was the brook of Ziba?
    A: Not close at all. Ziba was one of King Saul's servants— 2 Samuel 9:2
23. Who was the high priest when Nehemiah rebuilt the walls of Jerusalem?
    A: Eliashib—Nehemiah 3:1
24. How many men did Solomon use to cut stone for the temple?
    A: Eighty thousand (NIV)—1 Kings 5:15-17
25. The Bible says that what bird is cruel to her young?
    A: Ostrich—Job 39:13-17
26. God spoke to Jeremiah and said something that is a good argument against abortion. What was that statement?
    A: "Before I formed you in the womb, I knew you" (NIV) —Jeremiah 1:5
27. What was the name of Ezekiel's father?
    A: Buzi—Ezekiel 1:3
28. What Bible character thought laughter was a foolish thing?
    A: Solomon—Ecclesiastes 2:2
29. In what book of the Bible do you find the first mention of using battering rams against gates of a city?
    A: Ezekiel—Ezekiel 21:22
30. God showed a basket to the prophet Amos. What was in that basket?
    A: Fruit—Amos 8:1
31. The word eternity is used _____ times in the Bible.
    A: Once—Isaiah 57:15
32. Ahab's 70 sons had their heads cut off and sent in baskets to what man?
    A: Jehu—2 Kings 10:1-7

33. Which Bible character had the first king-sized bed?
    A: Og, king of Bashan—Deuteronomy 3:11
34. In which two books of the Bible do we read about cannibalism?
    A: 2 Kings and Lamentations—2 Kings 6:28,29; Lamentations 4:10
35. Which family in the Bible did not have to pay taxes?
    A: Jesse's family—1 Samuel 17:17,25,50
36. The Bible says that storks build their nests in what kind of trees?
    A: Pine (NIV); fir (KJV)—Psalm 104:17
37. How did God destroy the kings who attacked Gibeon?
    A: With hailstones—Joshua 10:5,11
38. In what book of the Bible does it talk about nose jewelry?
    A: Isaiah—Isaiah 3:21
39. What Bible character had his thumbs and big toes cut off by the tribes of Judah and Simeon?
    A: Adoni-Bezek—Judges 1:3-6
40. What Bible character hid his belt (girdle-KJV) in the crevice of the rocks?
    A: Jeremiah—Jeremiah 13:3-5
41. What is the name of the young virgin who kept King David warm during his old age?
    A: Abishag—1 Kings 1:1-3
42. King Saul sat under what kind of tree while Jonathan went to attack the Philistines?
    A: A pomegranate tree—1 Samuel 14:1,2
43. What was the name of Abraham's servant?
    A: Eliezer of Damascus—Genesis 15:2,3
44. How many chapters are there in the entire Bible?
    A: 1189
45. Who was the father of Ziddim, Zer, Hammath, Rakkath, and Kinnereth?
    A: No one. They were fortified cities—Joshua 19:35
46. How many chapters are there in the Old Testament?
    A: 929

47. What Bible character was beheaded, cremated, and then buried?
    A: King Saul—1 Samuel 31:8-13
48. In what book of the Bible do we find mention of "mufflers"?
    A: Isaiah—Isaiah 3:19
49. Gideon received golden earrings as payment for conquering the Midianites. How much did the earrings weigh?
    A: The same as 1700 shekels of gold—Judges 8:26
50. What is the most used word in the Bible?
    A: "The"
51. The valley of Siddim was famous for what?
    A: Tar pits (NIV); slimepits (KJV)—Genesis 14:10
52. Where was Ishbosheth's head buried?
    A: In Abner's tomb at Hebron—2 Samuel 4:12
53. When the tabernacle was built, who was the chief craftsman?
    A: Bezalel—Exodus 31:1-5
54. What emotion will cause your bones to rot?
    A: Envy—Proverbs 14:30
55. What group of people were told to burn their hair after it was cut off?
    A: The Nazarites—Numbers 6:18
56. Who was told to say, "My little finger is thicker than my father's waist" (NIV)?
    A: Rehoboam—2 Chronicles 10:6,7,10
57. In what book of the Bible do you find the "hill of the foreskins"?
    A: Joshua—Joshua 5:3
58. Hezekiah had a poultice put on his boil. What was the poultice made of?
    A: Figs—2 Kings 20:7
59. What was the name of Goliath's brother?
    A: Lahmi—1 Chronicles 20:5
60. What three things did the Pharisees and scribes tithe?
    A: Mint, dill (anise-KJV), cummin—Matthew 23:23

61. What are the names of the two women who had their ages recorded in the Bible?
    A: Sarah and Anna—Genesis 23:1; Luke 2:36,37
62. What was the name of the eunuch who was in charge of King Xerxes' (King Ahasuerus—KJV) concubines?
    A: Shaashgaz—Esther 2:12-14
63. What Bible character is mentioned as having an incurable bowel disease?
    A: Jehoram—2 Chronicles 21:18
64. What Bible character said that soldiers should be content with their pay?
    A: John the Baptist—Luke 3:14,15
65. The horses of the Babylonians (Chaldeans—KJV) were likened to what kind of animals?
    a. Lions b. Leopards c. Deer d. Sheep e. Eagles
    A: "B" or leopards—Habakkuk 1:6-8
66. What did Moses throw into the air to signal the start of the plague of boils on Egypt?
    A: Soot (NIV); ashes (KJV)—Exodus 9:8-10
67. In what book of the Bible do we find mention of "round tires like the moon"?
    A: Isaiah—Isaiah 3:18
68. In Zechariah's vision, the man on the red horse was riding among what kind of trees?
    A: Myrtle—Zechariah 1:8
69. What is the name of the man who tried to humiliate David's army by cutting off half of each soldier's beard and their garments in the middle at the buttocks?
    A: Hanun the Ammonite—2 Samuel 10:4
70. What is the name of the man who wrote Proverbs 30?
    A: Agur—Proverbs 30:1
71. In the book of Revelation, Antipas was martyred in _____ for his faith.
    A: Pergamum—Revelation 2:12,13
72. How many Bible characters are mentioned as living over 900 years?
    a. 3   b. 5   c. 7   d. 9   e. 11

A: "C" or 7—Genesis 5:5,8,11,14,20,27; 9:29

73. Solomon made the steps of the temple and the palace out of what kind of wood?
    A: Algum wood (NIV)—2 Chronicles 9:10,11

74. What were the first words Elisha spoke when he saw Elijah going to heaven?
    A: "My father, my father"—2 Kings 2:11,12

75. How many suicides are mentioned in the Bible?
    A: Seven

76. The wicked King Abimelech was critically injured by a woman dropping a_____on his head.
    A: Millstone—Judges 9:53

77. How many days was Ezekiel told to lie on his side while eating only bread and water?
    A: Three hundred and ninety—Ezekiel 4:9-11

78. King Asa had what kind of disease?
    A: A foot disease—2 Chronicles 16:12

79. God punished David for taking a census of the people. How many people died in God's punishment?
    A: Seventy thousand—1 Chronicles 21:1,14

80. The Israelites were told not to destroy what when they besieged cities in the Old Testament?
    A: The trees—Deuteronomy 20:19

81. How many shekels of silver did Achan steal?
    A: Two hundred—Joshua 7:20,21

82. The name Judas Iscariot appears how many times in the Bible?
    A: Ten

83. When Rachel stole some household gods from her father, she hid them in a camel's saddle and sat on the saddle. When her father came looking for the images, what excuse did Rachel use for not getting off the camel's saddle?
    A: She was having her period—Genesis 31:34,35

84. Obadiah hid _____ prophets in caves to protect them from Jezebel.
    A: One hundred—1 Kings 18:4

85. When the tower of Siloam fell, how many people were killed?
    A: Eighteen—Luke 13:4
86. What Bible character talks about beautiful feet?
    A: Isaiah—Isaiah 52:7
87. In what book of the Bible does it say, "Our skin was black like an oven because of the terrible famine"?
    A: Lamentations—Lamentations 5:10
88. In what book of the Bible do we find the famous verse, "At Parbar westward, four at the causeway, and two at Parbar"?
    A: 1 Chronicles—1 Chronicles 26:18
89. What Bible character cooked his bread on cow dung?
    A: Ezekiel—Ezekiel 4:15
90. Name the only book in the Bible that is addressed specifically to a woman.
    A: 2 John—2 John 1
91. How many people were shipwrecked with the apostle Paul in the book of Acts?
    A: Two hundred seventy-six—Acts 27:37,41
92. Who was the famous father of Maher-Shalel-Hash-Baz?
    A: Isaiah—Isaiah 8:3
93. What is the name of the king of Judah who made war machines that could shoot arrows and hurl huge stones?
    A: Uzziah—2 Chronicles 26:11,15
94. What was the name of Haman's wife?
    A: Zeresh—Esther 5:10,11
95. How many times does the name Satan appear in the Bible?
    A: Fifty-three
96. The manna in the wilderness was likened to what kind of seed?
    A: Coriander—Numbers 11:7
97. What will bring "health to thy navel and marrow to thy bones"?
    A: Fearing the Lord and departing from evil—Proverbs 3:7,8

98. Which town in the Bible had silver heaped up like dust and fine gold like the dirt of the streets?
    A: Tyre (NIV); Tyrus (KJV) — Zechariah 9:3

99. In what book of the Bible do we have mention of "sea monsters"?
    A: Lamentations — Lamentations 4:3

100. How many times is the word Lord mentioned in the Bible?
    a. 5,017 b. 6,370 c. 7,736 d. 8,212 e. 9,108
    A: "C" or 7,736

101. In what two books of the Bible does it talk about men drinking their own urine and eating their own refuse?
    A: 2 Kings and Isaiah — 2 Kings 18:27; Isaiah 36:12

102. Which book of the Bible mentions men "fearing lest they should fall into the quicksands"?
    A: Acts — Acts 27:17

103. To whom did Ebed-melech, the Ethiopian say, "Put now these . . . rotten rags under thine armholes"?
    A: Jeremiah — Jeremiah 38:12

104. What man in the Bible did not shave or wash his clothes for many days?
    A: Mephibosheth — 2 Samuel 19:24

105. Who grabbed Amasa by the beard with his right hand and pretended that he was going to kiss him, but instead stabbed him with a dagger?
    A: Joab — 2 Samuel 20:9,10

106. How many times is Beer mentioned in the Bible?
    A: Twice — Numbers 21:16; Judges 9:21

107. In what book of the Bible do we have the only mention of a ferry boat?
    A: 2 Samuel — 2 Samuel 19:18

108. What two tribes built an altar between them and called it Ed?
    A: Reuben and Gad — Joshua 22:34

109. Where in the Bible does it talk about a gathering of the sheriffs?
    A: Daniel — Daniel 3:2

110. In which book of the Bible does it talk about melting slugs or snails?
   A: Psalms—Psalm 58:8

111. How many times is the word "the" used in the Bible?
   a. Over 9,000   b. Over 11,000   c. Over 14,000
   d. Over 20,000
   A: "D" or over 20,000 times

112. In what book of the Bible do we find mention of stars singing?
   A: Job—Job 38:7

113. How many times is the word suburbs mentioned in the Bible?
   A: One hundred and fifteen

114. How many times are unicorns mentioned in the Bible?
   A: Nine—Numbers 23:22; 24:8; Deuteronomy 33:17; Job 39:9,10; Psalm 22:21; 29:6; 92:10; Isaiah 34:7

115. Who was the brother of Zered?
   A: No one. Zered was a valley (NIV) or brook (KJV)—Deuteronomy 2:13

116. If Cain was to be avenged sevenfold, how many times would Lamech be avenged?
   A: Seventy-seven—Genesis 4:24

117. To how many people did God say, "Be fruitful, and multiply, and replenish the earth"?
   A: Six—Adam, Eve, Noah, Shem, Ham, and Japheth—Genesis 1:28; 9:1

118. What time of day did God rain down fire and brimstone on Sodom and Gomorrah?
   A: Early in the morning—Genesis 19:23,24

119. What did Abraham call the name of the place where he was about to sacrifice Isaac?
   A: Jehovah-jireh, "the Lord will provide"—Genesis 22:14

120. How old was Esau when he married his two wives Judith and Basemath?
   A: Forty—Genesis 26:34

121. Isaiah prophesied that _____ women would take hold of one man.

A: Seven—Isaiah 4:1

122. Zechariah saw a vision of a scroll that was _____ feet long.

A: Thirty (twenty cubits)—Zechariah 5:1,2

123. Who was the first man to say, "I have sinned" in the Bible?

A: Pharaoh—Exodus 9:27

124. The Bible character Zaphenath-Paneah was known by another famous name. What was that name?

A: Joseph, son of Jacob—Genesis 41:45

125. In Zechariah's vision, the flying scroll was how wide?

A: Fifteen feet (ten cubits)—Zechariah 5:1,2

■ Answers to Puns, Riddles, and Humorous Trivia Questions

1. On the Ark, Noah probably got milk from the cows. What did he get from the ducks?
   A: Quackers
2. One of the first things Cain did after he left the Garden of Eden was to take a nap. How do we know this?
   A: Because he went to the land of Nod—Genesis 4:16
3. Where do you think the Israelites may have deposited their money?
   A: At the banks of the Jordan
4. Why do you think that the kangaroo was the most miserable animal on the Ark?
   A: Because her children had to play inside during the rain.
5. What prophet in the Bible was a space traveler?
   A: Elijah. He went up in a fiery chariot—2 Kings 2:11
6. What do you have that Cain, Abel, and Seth never had?
   A: Grandparents
7. What city in the Bible was named after something that you find on every modern-day car?
   A: Tyre (tire)
8. When the Ark landed on Mount Ararat, was Noah the first one out?

A: No, he came fourth out of the Ark.

9. What was the difference between the 10,000 soldiers of Israel and the 300 soldiers Gideon chose for battle?
   A: 9700

10. Where is the first math problem mentioned in the Bible?
    A: When God divided the light from the darkness.

11. Where is the second math problem mentioned in the Bible?
    A: When God told Adam and Eve to go forth and multiply—Genesis 1:28

12. Why did Noah have to punish and discipline the chickens on the Ark?
    A: Because they were using "fowl" language.

13. What was the most expensive meal served in the Bible and who ate it?
    A: Esau. It cost him his birthright—Genesis 25:34

14. Certain days in the Bible passed by more quickly than most of the days. Which days were these?
    A: The fast days

15. Matthew and Mark have something that is not found in Luke and John. What is it?
    A: The letter "a"

16. Which one of Noah's sons was considered to be a clown?
    A: His second son. He was always a Ham.

17. What was the first game mentioned in the Bible?
    A: When Adam and Eve played hide-and-seek with God.

18. What made Abraham so smart?
    A: He knew a Lot.

19. What is most of the time black, sometimes brown or white, but should be red?
    A: The Bible

20. Why did everyone on the Ark think that the horses were pessimistic?
    A: Because they always said neigh.

21. Who was the first person in the Bible to have surgery performed on him?
    A: Adam, when God removed one of his ribs—Genesis 2:21

22. When was the Red Sea very angry?
    A: When the children of Israel crossed it.
23. What vegetable did Noah not want on the Ark?
    A: Leeks
24. Why do you think Jonah could not trust the ocean?
    A: He knew that there was something fishy in it.
25. How do we know that God has a sense of humor?
    A: Because He can take a "rib."
26. What time was it when the hippopotamus sat on Noah's rocking chair?
    A: Time to get a new chair.
27. What does God both give away and keep at the same time?
    A: His promises
28. During the six days of creation, which weighed more—the day or the night?
    A: The night, because the day was light.
29. What did the skunks on the Ark have that no other animals had?
    A: Baby skunks
30. What type of tea does the Bible suggest that we not drink?
    A: Vanity (vani-tea)
31. In what book of the Bible do we find something that is in modern-day courtrooms?
    A: Judges
32. Which animal on the Ark was the rudest?
    A: The mockingbird
33. What kind of soap did God use to keep the oceans clean?
    A. Tide
34. How do we know that the disciples were very cruel to the corn?
    A: Because they pulled its ears.
35. Why did the rooster refuse to fight on the Ark?
    A: Because he was chicken.
36. Why didn't Cain please the Lord with his offering?
    A: He simply wasn't Abel.

37. One of the names of the books of the Bible contains an
    insect in it. Which one is it?
    A: Ti-(moth)-y
38. How many animals could Noah put into the empty Ark?
    A: One. After that the Ark would not be empty.
39. Which man in the Bible might have only been 12 inches?
    A: Nicodemus, because he was a ruler—John 3:1
40. Which book in the Bible is the counting book?
    A: Numbers
41. What kind of lights did Noah have on the Ark?
    A: Flood lights
42. Gideon had 70 sons. How many of them were big men
    when they were born?
    A: None of them. They were all babies.
43. Which candle burns longer—the candle hidden under
    a bushel or the candle set on a hill?
    A: Neither one. They both burn shorter.
44. Which animal on Noah's Ark had the highest level of
    intelligence?
    A: The giraffe
45. What indication is there that there may have been news-
    paper reporters in the New Testament?
    A: Because Zaccheus couldn't see Jesus "for the press"
    —Luke 19:3
46. The name of one book of the Bible contains an ugly
    old woman. Which book is it?
    A: (Hag)-gai
47. Which animal on the Ark did Noah not trust?
    A: The cheetah
48. Which Bible character was as strong as steel?
    A: Iron—Joshua 19:38
49. What man in the Bible is named after a chicken?
    A: Hen—Zechariah 6:14
50. Where does the Bible suggest that it is okay to be over-
    weight?
    A: Leviticus 3:16—"All the fat is the Lord's."

51. What Bible character had a name that rang a bell?
    A: Mehetabel (Ma-hit-a-bell)—Nehemiah 6:10
52. Which bird on Noah's Ark was a thief?
    A: A robin
53. Where does the Bible suggest that newspapers, magazines, radio, and television are powerful?
    A: Esther 1:3—"The power of Persia and Media. . . ."
54. What is the name of the individual who was perfect in the Bible?
    A: Mark—Psalm 37:37: "Mark the perfect man, and behold the upright."
55. What was Eve's formal name?
    A: Madam Adam
56. On Noah's Ark, why did the dog have so many friends?
    A: Because he wagged his tail instead of his tongue.
57. Who killed a fourth of all the people in the world?
    A: Cain when he killed Abel—Genesis 4:1,2,8
58. Where does it suggest that there may have been buses in the Bible?
    A: In Proverbs 30:31 where it talks about the greyhound.
59. When Eve left the garden without Adam, what did Adam say?
    A: Eve is absent without leaf.
60. When a camel with no hump was born on the Ark, what did Noah name it?
    A: Humphrey
61. How long did Samson love Delilah?
    A: Until she bald him out.
62. Where were freeways first mentioned in the Bible?
    A: Genesis 1:30—"The Lord made every creeping thing."
63. What is the name of the sleepiest land in the Bible?
    A: The land of Nod—Genesis 4:16
64. What did Noah call the cat that fell into the pickle barrel on the Ark?
    A: A sour puss

65. What age were the goats when Adam named them in the Garden of Eden?
   A: They were only kids.
66. David played a dishonest musical instrument. What was it called?
   A: The lyre
67. Which of the Old Testament prophets were blind?
   A: Ezra, Hosea, Joel, Amos, Jonah, Nahum, Habakkuk. None of them have i's.
68. How did Noah keep the milk from turning sour on the Ark?
   A: He left it in the cow.
69. How many books in the Old Testament were named after Esther?
   A: Twenty-two—The rest were named before Esther.
70. What would have happened if all the women would have left the nation of Israel?
   A: It would have been a stagnation.
71. Why did the giant fish finally let Jonah go?
   A: He couldn't stomach him.
72. Why was Moses buried in a valley in the land of Moab near Bethpeor?
   A: Because he was dead.
73. The name of a book of the Bible contains a fruit. Which book is it?
   A: Phi-(lemon)
74. What is in the wall of Jerusalem that the Israelites did not put there?
   A: Cracks
75. Why was "W" the nastiest letter in the Bible?
   A: Because it always makes ill will.
76. How did Joseph learn to tell the naked truth?
   A: By exposing the bare facts.
77. What food did Samson eat to become strong?
   A: Mussels
78. Why did the tower of Babel stand in the land of Shinar?
   A: Because it couldn't sit down.

79. Why did Moses have to be hidden quickly when he was a baby?
    A: Saving him was a rush job.
80. Where in the Bible do we find the authority for women to kiss men?
    A: Matthew 7:12—"Whatsoever ye would that men should do to you, do ye even so to them."
81. What two things could Samson the Nazarite never eat for breakfast?
    A: Lunch and supper
82. If Elijah was invited to dinner and was served only a beet, what would he say?
    A: That beet's all.
83. If a man crosses the Sea of Galilee twice without a bath, what would he be?
    A: A dirty double-crosser
84. If someone wanted to be converted by John the Baptist, what was the first requirement?
    A: You had to go from bad to immerse.
85. What day of the week was the best for cooking manna in the wilderness?
    A: Friday
86. If a soft answer turneth away wrath, what does a hard answer do?
    A: It turneth wrath your way.
87. In what book of the Bible does it talk about people wearing tires on their heads?
    A: Ezekiel—Ezekiel 24:23
88. What is the golden rule of the animal world?
    A: Do unto otters as you would have them do unto you.
89. How did Adam and Eve feel when they left the garden?
    A: A little put out.
90. Samson was a very strong man but there was one thing he could not hold for very long. What was that?
    A: His breath

91. If Moses would have dropped his rod in the Red Sea,
    what would it have become?
    A: Wet

92. What fur did Adam and Eve wear?
    A: Bareskin

93. Why must Elijah's parents have been good business
    people?
    A: Because they made a prophet.

94. Jesus and the giant fish that swallowed Jonah have some-
    thing in common. What is it?
    A: Jesus had dinner with a sinner and the giant fish had
    a sinner for dinner.

95. What did Joseph in the Old Testament have in common
    with Zaccheus in the New Testament?
    A: Joseph's job was *overseeing*, and Zaccheus' problem
    was *seeing over*.

96. In what way does an attorney resemble a rabbi?
    A: The attorney studies the law and the profits.

97. What does a Christian man love more than life;
    Hate more than death or mortal strife;
    That which contented men desire;
    The poor have, the rich require;
    The miser spends, the spendthrift saves;
    And all men carry to their graves?
    A: Nothing

98. What is that which Adam never saw or possessed, yet left
    two for each of his children?
    A: Parents

99. What is greater than God, not as wicked as Satan, if peo-
    ple are alive and eat it they will die, and dead people eat it?
    A: Nothing